It's another Quality Book from CGP

This book has been carefully written for
children working towards a Level 4.

It matches the Attainment Targets perfectly.

There's lots of stuff to learn if you want to get a Level 4.
Happily this CGP book explains all the important information
as clearly and simply as possible.

It's also got some daft bits in to try and make the whole experience
at least vaguely entertaining for you.

What CGP is all about

Our sole aim here at CGP is to produce the highest quality books
— carefully written, immaculately presented and
dangerously close to being funny.

Then we work our socks off to get them out to you
— at the cheapest possible prices.

Contents

SECTION FOUR — UNDERSTANDING SHAPE

SECTION FIVE — MEASURING

SECTION SIX — HANDLING DATA

SECTION SEVEN — USING AND APPLYING MATHEMATICS

Published by Coordination Group Publications Ltd.

Editors:
Jane Aston, Charlotte Burrows, Katherine Craig, Charley Darbishire, Sarah Hilton, Sharon Keeley,
Rob MacDonald, Hannah Nash, Andy Park, Julie Wakeling, Sarah Williams.

Key Stage Two Consultant:
John Cullen

ISBN: 978 1 84762 195 5

With thanks to Ali Palin, Teresa Cowell and Mary McNama for the proofreading.

Groovy website: www.cgpbooks.co.uk

With thanks to Jan Greenway for the copyright research.
Thumb illustration used throughout the book © iStockphoto.com.

Printed by Elanders Hindson Ltd, Newcastle upon Tyne.
Jolly bits of clipart from CorelDRAW®

About the Book

This Book has *All the Tricky Topics for Level 4*

You've got a good chance of getting a <u>Level 4</u> if you can do <u>all the maths</u> in this book.

There are a couple of pages on each topic.
One page <u>explains</u> the maths.
The other page has <u>worked examples</u>.
These show you how to answer questions.

> This book covers all the
> <u>Attainment Targets</u> for Level 4.
> They say what maths children
> working at Level 4 can usually do.

There are *Practice Questions for Each Section*

At the end of each section are <u>practice questions</u>.
You can see what you know and what you don't know.

There's a <u>matching Level 4 Question Book</u>.
It's got questions on all the topics.
It also has some practice tests too.

> I love to practise.
> I love to practise.

There are *Learning Objectives on All Pages*

Learning Objectives say <u>what you need to know</u>.
Use the <u>tick circles</u> to show how well you understand the maths.
Use a pencil. You can <u>tick other circles</u> as you get better.

> I can win gold
> at the Olympics.

> Tick here if you can do some
> of the Learning Objective.

> If you're struggling,
> tick here.

> Tick this circle if you can do the
> Learning Objective really well.

Learning Objective:

"I can name polygons. I can say whether a triangle is
equilateral, isosceles or scalene and explain how I know."

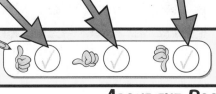

Decimals

Decimals are one way to write numbers that <u>aren't whole numbers</u>.

Decimals — the Basics

<u>Whole numbers</u> have Units, Tens, Hundreds and so on.

<u>Decimal numbers</u> also have <u>tenths</u>, <u>hundredths</u> and <u>thousandths</u>...

| u | t | h | th |

2.001   is just a bit bigger than 2

2.983   is just a bit less than 3

2.500   is halfway between 2 and 3

Remember, you can partition decimals.
For example, **2.983** = 2 + 0.9 + 0.08 + 0.003

You can see where decimals are on a <u>number line</u>:

"Can't we just forget these ones?"

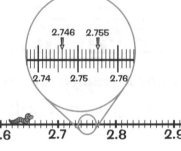

Ordering Decimals

Five Steps to Decimal Heaven

1) Arrange all the numbers in <u>place value columns</u>.
(Make sure all the decimal points are <u>underneath</u> each other.)

2) Make them all the <u>same length</u> by filling in extra zeros.

3) Look at the <u>whole number</u> part of each decimal number.
Arrange the numbers from smallest to largest.

4) If any whole numbers are the same, look at the digits in the <u>tenths</u> column. Arrange them from smallest to largest.

5) If any of the tenths are the same, look at the digits in the <u>hundredths</u> column. Arrange them from smallest to largest.

Just do the same again with thousandths if there are any.

EXAMPLE: Order these numbers from smallest to largest: 0.7 1.02 0.29 0.23

STEP 1:	STEP 2:	STEP 3:	STEP 4:	STEP 5:
0.7	0.70	0.70	0.29	0.23
1.02	1.02	0.29	0.23	0.29
0.29	0.29	0.23	0.70	0.70
0.23	0.23	1.02	1.02	1.02

Learning Objective:

ANSWER: 0.23, 0.29, 0.7, 1.02

"I can use decimals with up to three places, order them, and put them on a number line."

Decimals

Question 1

Draw an arrow to show **76.18** on this number line.

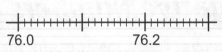

① __Partition__ the number first:

② The whole number part is **76**.
The first digit after the __decimal point__ is the __tenths__. The second digit after the decimal point is the __hundredths__.

③ Find 76.<u>1</u> on the number line...

④ ...then count on <u>8 hundredths</u>.

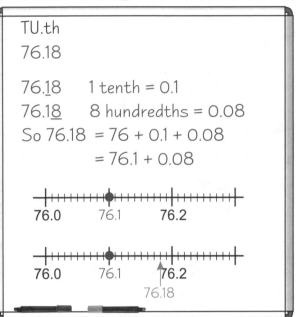

TU.th
76.18

76.1<u>8</u>   1 tenth = 0.1
76.1<u>8</u>   8 hundredths = 0.08
So 76.18 = 76 + 0.1 + 0.08
              = 76.1 + 0.08

Question 2

Jim weighs three pieces of pasta. They have masses of **1.275 g**, **1.07 g** and **1.273 g**. Put the masses in order, beginning with the **smallest**.

① Arrange the numbers in __place value columns__ with the decimal points lined up. Make all the numbers the __same length__ by filling in __extra zeros__.

② The units digits are __all the same__ (1). So compare the __tenths__ digits. 1.<u>2</u>73 and 1.<u>2</u>75 are larger than 1.<u>0</u>70, so 1.070 comes first.

③ Next, look at the __hundredths__. 1.2<u>7</u>3 and 1.2<u>7</u>5 both have 7 hundredths, so you need to look at the __thousandths__. 1.27<u>5</u> is larger than 1.27<u>3</u>, so 1.273 comes before 1.275.

④ Remember to put the __units of measurement__ (grams) in your answer.

1.275
1.070
1.273

1.070
1.275
1.273

1.070   1.070
1.275 ⟶ 1.273
1.273   1.275

So the order is:
1.07 g, 1.273 g, 1.275 g

Whole numbers, _then tenths,_ _then hundredths,_ then thousandths...

Decimals aren't as bad as they look — you just need to <u>practise</u>. Test yourself by writing down some decimals and putting them in order. Then put them all on a number line.

Numbers and Number Lines

Negative Numbers are Less than Zero

The <u>number line</u> is really useful for understanding <u>negative numbers</u>.

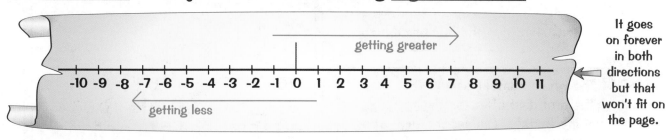

getting greater

getting less

-10 -9 -8 -7 -6 -5 -4 -3 -2 -1 0 1 2 3 4 5 6 7 8 9 10 11

It goes on forever in both directions but that won't fit on the page.

The further <u>right</u> you go, the <u>greater</u> the numbers get.
All <u>negative numbers</u> are to the <u>left of zero</u>.
All <u>positive numbers</u> are to the <u>right of zero</u>.

Use < and > to Compare Numbers

Inequalities use the symbols < and >.
　　For example, 5 > 2 means
　　　　'5 is greater than 2'.

< means 'is less than'
> means 'is greater than'

EXAMPLE: Put the correct <u>inequality symbol</u> in each box.

6 ☐ –1　⟹　6 is greater than –1, so　6 > –1

–5 ☐ –3　⟹　–5 is less than –3, so　–5 < –3

It's easy to think that -5 is greater than -3 because 5 is greater than 3.
But <u>-5</u> is <u>less</u> than <u>-3</u> because it's <u>further away from 0</u> on the <u>less than 0</u> side of the number line.

Use a Number Line to Work out Differences

EXAMPLE: In London the temperature is <u>–2 °C</u>. In Paris it's <u>12 °C</u>.
What is the <u>difference</u> in temperature between the two places?

Count on from –2 to 12.

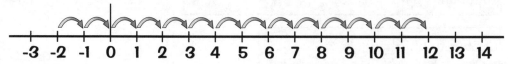

-3 -2 -1 0 1 2 3 4 5 6 7 8 9 10 11 12 13 14

There are 14 steps so the difference in temperature is <u>14 °C</u>.

Learning Objective:

"I can place positive and negative numbers on a number line and use inequality signs."

SECTION ONE — COUNTING AND UNDERSTANDING NUMBER

Numbers and Number Lines

Question 1

The temperature outside Jan's house is **–18 °C**. Inside it is **21 °C**.
What is the difference between these two temperatures? Show your working.

1 Draw a <u>number line</u> that includes the highest and lowest numbers in the question.
For this one I've started at –20 and gone up to 21.

2 Use the number line to <u>count on</u> in <u>easy steps</u> from –18 to 21.

3 <u>Add up</u> all the steps. Remember to put the <u>unit</u> in your final answer.

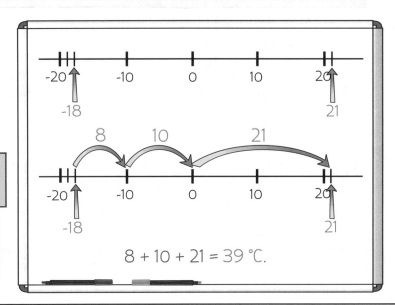

$$8 + 10 + 21 = 39 \text{ °C.}$$

Question 2

Here are four numbers. **8**, **3**, **7**, **1**
Write one number in each box to make the following number sentences correct.
You should only use the numbers once.

a) ☐ – 3 > 2   b) ☐ × 2 < 10 – ☐

a) **1** When you subtract three from the missing number, the answer must be <u>greater than 2</u>.

2 Try each of the possible numbers. Start with 8.

b) **1** Try putting numbers in the boxes. (Remember, you can't use 8 if you used it in part a.)

2 <u>Work out the calculations</u> and see if the number sentence is <u>true</u>. Try different combinations until you get one that works.

$? – 3 > 2$

$8 – 3 = \underline{5}$, and 5 is greater than 2
So an answer is: $8 – 3 > 2$
    ($\underline{7} – 3 > 2$ also works)

$3 × 2 < 10 – 7$
    $\underline{6} \ < \ \underline{3}$, which is not true

$1 × 2 < 10 – 7$
    $\underline{2} \ < \ \underline{3}$, which is true
So an answer is $1 × 2 \ < \ 10 – 7$
    ($\underline{1} × 2 < 10 – \underline{3}$ and
    $\underline{3} × 2 < 10 – \underline{1}$ also work)

< and > mean 'less than' and 'greater than'...

It's easy to get < and > mixed up. But here's a way to remember them — the <u>wider end</u> of the symbol goes next to the <u>greater number</u>. So for example, 5 > 4, or –3 < 4.

Percentages

"Per Cent" Means "Out of 100"

% is a short way of writing <u>per cent</u> and it just means "out of 100".

So 20% is twenty per cent, which is <u>20 out of 100</u> (or 20 parts in every 100).

You can write any percentage as a <u>fraction</u>.

Put the <u>percentage</u> on the <u>top</u> and <u>100</u> on the <u>bottom</u> of the fraction.

EXAMPLE: $20\% = \dfrac{20}{100}$

You Can Convert *Fractions into Percentages*

Changing fractions into percentages is mostly OK.

Converting Hundredths is Easy

<u>Hundredths</u> are already "out of a hundred".

So the <u>numerator</u> (top number) is the <u>percentage</u>. It's as simple as that.

$\dfrac{55}{100} = 55\%$

$\dfrac{30}{100} = 30\%$

$\dfrac{6}{100} = 6\%$

For Tenths, Make an Equivalent Fraction

<u>Tenths</u> are "out of ten", not "out of a hundred".

So you have to make an <u>equivalent fraction</u> with <u>100 as the denominator</u>.

Just <u>multiply</u> the denominator and numerator by <u>10</u>.

bottom number

EXAMPLE:

Write six tenths as a percentage.

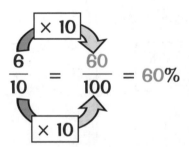

$\dfrac{6}{10} = \dfrac{60}{100} = 60\%$

They all follow the same pattern.

$\dfrac{9}{10} = \dfrac{90}{100} = 90\%$

And make sure you <u>learn</u> these ones...

$\dfrac{1}{10} = 10\%$ $\dfrac{1}{4} = 25\%$ $\dfrac{1}{2} = 50\%$ $\dfrac{3}{4} = 75\%$

Learning Objective:

"I know that 'per cent' means 'parts in every 100'.

I can give a simple fraction as a percentage."

Percentages

Question 1

Harry's Dad makes him a birthday cake. Harry eats $\frac{2}{10}$ of the cake.

How much of the cake is left? Give your answer as a percentage.

1 Convert 2 tenths into a percentage. Make an equivalent fraction that has 100 as the denominator.

2 So Harry eats 20% of the cake. The whole cake was 100%. Now you can work out how much cake is left.

$$\frac{2}{10} = \frac{20}{100} = 20\%$$

$$100\% - 20\% = 80\%$$
80% of the cake is left.

Question 2

Tom did a Maths test. He got four out of ten.
His older sister Katie also did a Maths test. She scored 36 out of a hundred.
Who scored the higher percentage in their Maths test?

1 Write both scores as fractions.

2 Convert Tom's score into a percentage.

3 Write Katie's score as a percentage.

4 Then just compare the two percentages.

Tom scored $\frac{4}{10}$ Katie scored $\frac{36}{100}$

$$\frac{4}{10} = \frac{40}{100} = 40\%$$

$$\frac{36}{100} = 36\%$$

40% > 36%
So Tom scored the higher percentage.

Practise changing fractions into percentages...

Remember, a percentage is a number "out of a hundred". To write a fraction as a percentage, just make an equivalent fraction that has 100 as the denominator.

Proportion and Ratio

"For Every" Questions

EXAMPLE: Matt and Nic are eating pizza.
Matt eats 2 slices of pizza for every 1 that Nic eats.

Another way to say this is:
'They share the pizza in the ratio 2:1.'

<u>This means that:</u>
There are 3 shares of pizza in total. For every
1 share that Nic gets, Matt gets 2 shares.

So Nic has $\frac{1}{3}$ of the total number of slices and Matt has $\frac{2}{3}$ of the total number.

Nic's share

Matt's share

You can show this using <u>sequences</u>.
Matt eats <u>twice</u> as many slices as Nic.
So if Nic eats 4 slices, Matt eats 8 slices.

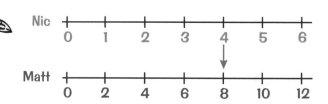

"In Every" Questions

EXAMPLE: In 'Chocowasp' chocolate boxes, 1 in every 4 chocolates is a wasp cream.
Tony buys a box of 20 chocolates. How many wasp creams will he get?

The <u>proportion</u> of wasp creams is <u>1 in every 4</u>.

'<u>1 in every 4</u>' means that $\frac{1}{4}$ of the chocolates are wasp creams.

So find $\frac{1}{4}$ of <u>20 chocolates</u>. That's <u>20 ÷ 4 = 5 wasp creams</u>.

You Can Scale Recipes Up or Down

EXAMPLE: A recipe for 2 people uses 3 daffodils and 2 eggs.

a) Gary puts 6 eggs in. How many daffodils does he need?

6 eggs is 3 times as many eggs as in the recipe.
So he needs 3 times as many daffodils too. $3 \times 3 = 9$ daffodils.

b) How many eggs and daffodils would he need for 8 people?

He needs 4 times as many ingredients for 8 people as he does for 2.
So he will need $3 \times 4 = 12$ daffodils and $2 \times 4 = 8$ eggs.

Learning Objective:

"I can use the relationships between numbers to solve
ratio and proportion questions."

Proportion and Ratio

Question 1

Helen is making orange drink. She mixes 4 parts water to 1 part squash.
a) What fraction of the drink will be water?
b) Helen wants to make 500 ml of orange drink. How much squash does she need?

a) 1. Write down the 'recipe'. There are 5 parts altogether.
2. Water is 4 parts out of 5.

b) 1. Squash is 1 part out of 5.
2. Find one fifth of 500 ml.

4 parts water to 1 part squash
4 parts + 1 part = 5 parts

$\frac{4}{5}$ of the drink is water.

$\frac{1}{5}$ of the drink is squash.

500 ml ÷ 5 = 100 ml of squash.

Question 2

Amy is making brownies. Part of the recipe is shown on the right.
a) Amy makes the brownies using 10 eggs. How many pieces of chocolate will she need?
b) Ben wants to make brownies for 12 people. How many eggs and pieces of chocolate will he need?

For 3 people
2 eggs
6 pieces of chocolate...

a) 1. Amy is using 10 eggs. The recipe uses 2 eggs.
2. Scale the pieces of chocolate up by the same number.

b) 1. Ben is making brownies for 12 people. The recipe is for 3 people.
2. Multiply the quantities of eggs and pieces of chocolate by 4.

10 eggs is 5 times as many as 2 eggs.

The recipe uses 6 pieces of chocolate.
6 × 5 = 30 pieces of chocolate

12 is 4 times as many as 3, so Ben needs to multiply the ingredients by 4.

2 × 4 = 8 eggs
6 × 4 = 24 pieces of chocolate

It's not always a recipe...

Try this: "Two apples cost 30p. How much do five apples cost?" (You have to scale down first, to find the cost of one apple. Then scale that up to find the cost of five apples.)

Answer: 1 apple costs 30 ÷ 2 = 15p. 5 apples cost 15 × 5 = 75p.

SECTION ONE — COUNTING AND UNDERSTANDING NUMBER

Practice Questions

1   Partition 2.658 into units, tenths, hundredths and thousandths.

2.658 = ☐ + ☐ + ☐ + ☐

2   Peter runs the 100 m race in 14.45 s.
Michael takes one tenth of a second longer.

What is Michael's time?

3   Look at this number line.

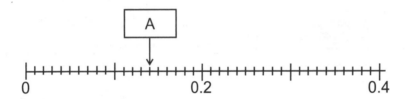

A

0   0.2   0.4

a)   What decimal number is the arrow A pointing to?

b)   Copy the number line. Draw an arrow pointing to 0.37.

4   Four snails race across a leaf.
Their times are recorded in the table.

Write these times in order from fastest to slowest.

Snail	Time (s)
1	5.932
2	5.99
3	5.930
4	6.01

5   Frank and Jeremy both went on a TV gameshow.
Frank scored −12 points and Jeremy scored −9 points.

Whose score was higher, and by how many points?

6   Copy these number sentences and put the correct inequality sign in each box.

One has been done for you.

−5 > −7   a) 6 ☐ 2   b) −3 ☐ −1   c) 2.3 ☐ 2.5

Practice Questions

7   Inside the Ice Hotel it is –6 °C. Outside it is 3 °C.

What is the difference in temperature between the inside and the outside?

8   Sarah played 10 tennis matches. She won 8 of them.

What percentage of her matches did she win?

9   Mrs Jones gave both her children the same amount of porridge for breakfast.

Katherine ate $\frac{1}{4}$ of her porridge. Janet ate 20% of her porridge.

Who ate more porridge? Show your method.

10   Dave has twice as many blue socks as red socks.
He has 60 socks in total.

How many blue socks does Dave have?

11   Charlotte buys three eggs for 90p.

How much would four eggs cost?

12   Bob wants to make some cakes. He finds this recipe.

> Recipe for 12 cakes:
>
> 150 g flour
> 75 g sugar
> 75 g margarine
> 3 eggs

a)   Bob only has 1 egg.
How many cakes can he make?

b)   Bob decides to buy some more ingredients. He wants to makes 36 cakes.
How much margarine does he need?

Checking Calculations

It's easy to make mistakes. So you should always <u>check your answers</u>.

Do the Inverse Operation...

EXAMPLE: Fred works out <u>72 − 32</u>. His answer is 50.
He can <u>check</u> it by doing the <u>inverse operation</u>.

> **Inverse** just means <u>opposite</u>.

The inverse of "<u>− 32</u>" is "<u>+ 32</u>".
Fred should do <u>50 + 32</u> and see if he gets <u>72</u>.

> **ADDITION** and **SUBTRACTION** are <u>inverse operations</u>.

$$50 + 32 = \underline{82}$$

Fred was expecting to get <u>72</u>, so his answer of 50 <u>must be wrong</u>.

> **MULTIPLICATION** and **DIVISION** are <u>inverse operations</u>.

...Or Estimate by Rounding Up or Down

You can check an answer by comparing it to an <u>estimate</u>.

EXAMPLE: Mary works out that <u>38 + 49</u> = <u>87</u>.
To check this, she can do an estimate to get a <u>rough answer</u>.

Round each number in the sum to the nearest 10.

> 38 is about 40.
> 49 is about 50

Add the rounded numbers together. → 40 + 50 = 90

So → 38 + 49 is <u>about 90</u>

> I'm only 87...

So Mary's answer of <u>87</u> seems <u>fine</u>.
It's <u>probably right</u>.

Check that Your Answer is Sensible

Always <u>read your answer</u> and see if it <u>makes sense</u>.

"The <u>bus</u> is <u>2.5 m</u> high."   ← This is <u>OK</u>.

The <u>pencil</u> is <u>2 m</u> long.

This <u>can't be right</u>.
You don't get 2-metre long pencils.

Learning Objective:

"I can check the result of a calculation."

Checking Calculations

Question 1

Sanjay has done the calculations shown to the right.
Check his answers by using inverse operations.
Show your method and write 'correct' or 'incorrect' for each one.

a) $19 + 28 = 47$
b) $63 - 33 = 23$
c) $18 \times 6 = 108$
d) $199 \div 19 = 11$

1 For each calculation, start with Sanjay's <u>answer</u> and write the <u>inverse operation</u>.

For example, for a), start with <u>47</u> and write the inverse of '+ 28'. So it's 47 <u>– 28</u>.

2 Do each calculation.

3 If your answer <u>matches</u> the numbers in the original calculation then Sanjay was <u>correct</u>.

a) $47 - 28$ (Or you could do 47 – 19, because 19 + 28 is the same as 28 + 19.)

b) $23 + 33$

c) $108 \div 6$ (Or you could do 108 ÷ 18, because 18 × 6 is the same as 6 × 18.)

d) 11×19

a) $47 - 28 = 19$ correct
b) $23 + 33 = 56$ not 63, so incorrect
c) $108 \div 6 = 18$ correct
d) $11 \times 19 = 209$ not 199, so incorrect

Question 2

Emma has done three calculations.

A $28 + 89 = 145$ **B** $12.1 - 8.7 = 3.4$ **C** $18.8 \times 2.2 = 41.36$

Use estimation to check her answers.
Write **probably right** or **probably wrong** for each one. Show your working.

1 <u>Round the numbers</u> up or down to the nearest ten or the nearest whole number.

2 Work out the answer to each estimate. If your estimated answer is <u>close</u> to Emma's answer, Emma was <u>probably right</u>.

A   28 + 89 is about <u>30 + 90</u>
B   12.1 – 8.7 is about <u>12 – 9</u>
C   18.8 × 2.2 is about <u>20 × 2</u>

A   30 + 90 = <u>120</u> Probably wrong
B   12 – 9 = <u>3</u> Probably right
C   20 × 2 = <u>40</u> Probably right

Use rounding to estimate and check your answers...

<u>Always</u> check your answers. One way is to use the <u>inverse</u> operation. Or you can <u>round</u> up or down to make a simpler calculation. And finally, check that your answer is <u>sensible</u>.

Factors and Multiples

Factors of a Number

The <u>factors</u> of a number are whole numbers that <u>divide exactly into</u> that number. (<u>Two factors</u> will <u>multiply together</u> to give the number.)

> The number 10 has factors 1, 10, 2 and 5
> because $1 \times 10 = 10$ and $2 \times 5 = 10$
>
> The number 12 has factors 1, 12, 2, 6, 3 and 4
> because $1 \times 12 = 12$, $2 \times 6 = 12$ and $3 \times 4 = 12$

A number is <u>divisible</u> (can be divided exactly) by all its factors. For example, 10 is <u>divisible</u> by 1, 10, 2 and 5.

Factors written like this
(3×4)
are known as <u>factor pairs</u>.

Multiples are Just Like Times Tables

So the <u>multiples of 2</u> are just the numbers in the <u>2 times table</u>:

2	4	6	8	10	12	14	16	...

The <u>multiples of 8</u> are   8   16   24   32   40   48   ...

The <u>multiples of 12</u> are   12   24   36   48   60   72   84   ...

It's easy to remember:
MULTIPLes are just
MULTIPLication tables.

Finding Common Multiples

A <u>common multiple</u> of two numbers is a number that's a <u>multiple of both numbers</u>. You can find them by <u>listing times tables</u>.

EXAMPLE: Find a <u>common multiple</u> of 6 and 8.

1) Write out the <u>6 times table</u>...
(Go up to 5×6 to start with.)   ⟶   6   12   18   24   30

2) ...then the <u>8 times table</u>.   ⟶   8   16   24   ...

3) Look out for a number that's <u>in both lists</u>. When you find one, it's a common multiple.
(There are lots, but you only need one for this question, so stop here.)

So a common multiple of 6 and 8 is <u>24</u>.

Learning Objective:

"I can find pairs of factors that multiply to make a given number. I can find a common multiple of two numbers."

Factors and Multiples

Question 1

Write down all the factor pairs of 24.

① You have to find all the factors of 24.

Start at 1 and go through the whole numbers (1, 2, 3, 4,...) asking yourself, "Does this number divide exactly into 24?"

② For each factor you find, write down how many times the factor goes into 24.
For example 4 × 6 = 24.
So 4 × 6 is one of the factor pairs.

③ List all the factors in pairs.

The factors of 24 are:

1, 2, 3, 4, 5̶, 6, 7̶, 8, 9̶, 1̶0̶, 1̶1̶, 12, 1̶3̶, 1̶4̶,
1̶5̶, 1̶6̶, 1̶7̶, 1̶8̶, 1̶9̶, 2̶0̶, 2̶1̶, 2̶2̶, 2̶3̶, 24

$$1, \quad 2, \quad 3, \quad 4, \quad 6$$
× 24   × 8   × 4
      × 12   × 6

(6 × 4 is the same as 4 × 6, so stop here. If you carry on you'll just repeat more pairs you've already got.)

So the factor pairs of 24 are:
1 × 24, 2 × 12, 3 × 8, 4 × 6

Question 2

Find a common multiple of 10 and 12.

① Start to write out the 10 and 12 times tables.

② Find a number that appears in both lists. This is a common multiple.

10 times table:
10, 20, 30, 40, 50, 60, 70

12 times table:
12, 24, 36, 48, 60, 72, 84

10, 20, 30, 40, 50, 60, 70
12, 24, 36, 48, 60, 72, 84

A common multiple of 10 and 12 is 60.

Don't get factors and multiples muddled up....

Remember, factors come in pairs that multiply together to make a number.
The multiples of a number are just numbers in the times table of that number.

Multiplication and Division

You can Multiply in Any Order

You can say:

2 rows of 3 apples...  ... or 3 columns of 2 apples

2×3 3×2

... but the answer is still 6.

EXAMPLE: Jack plants 6 magic bean seeds in every pot.
He has 9 pots. How many seeds does he plant?

You need to work out $6 \times 9 = ?$

You can get the answer using the 6 times table  $9 \times 6 = 6 \times 9 = 54$
or the 9 times table. It doesn't matter which.

Dividing is just Sharing

15 "divided by" **3**, 15 "shared by" **3**, **3** "into" 15 "goes"...
...all mean the same thing.

You can also think of $15 \div 3$ as putting 15 things into 3 equal groups.

Dividing is the Inverse of Multiplying

Multiply 3 by 6 and you get 18. $3 \times 6 = 18$

Divide 18 by 6 and you get 3 again. $18 \div 6 = 3$

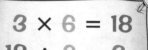 You can use your times tables to help you divide.

EXAMPLE: Divide fifty-six by seven.

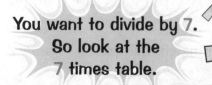 You want to divide by 7.
So look at the
7 times table.

$56 \div 7 = ?$

$8 \times 7 = 56$

So ⟶ $56 \div 7 = 8$

Learning Objective:

"I know my times tables to 10×10."   

Multiplication and Division

Question 1

Chris is about to feed the monkeys at the zoo. Each monkey gets 7 pieces of fruit.
There are 9 monkeys. How many pieces of fruit will Chris need?

1 Work out <u>what calculation</u> you need to do.

2 Use a <u>times table</u> to work out the answer.

Each monkey gets 7 pieces of fruit.

There are 9 monkeys, so Chris will need 9 lots of 7 pieces of fruit.

So you need to <u>multiply</u>: 7×9 or 9×7.

$7 \times 9 = 9 \times 7 = 63$ pieces of fruit.

Question 2

Rick sells flowers in bunches of 6. He has 55 flowers.
How many bunches can he make altogether?

1 Work out <u>what calculation</u> you need to do.

2 You want to divide by 6, so look at the <u>6 times table</u>.

55 isn't a multiple of 6, so look for a multiple of 6 that's <u>just less than 55</u>.

3 Now work out <u>how many bunches</u> Rick can make from <u>54 flowers</u>. You need to <u>divide</u>. Use the <u>inverse</u> to help you find the answer.

Rick has to share the 55 flowers out in groups of 6. You need to <u>divide</u>.

$$55 \div 6 = ?$$

The 6 times table is
6, 12, 18, 24, 30, 36, 42, 48, (54) 60,...

Rick can only use 54 flowers.
He will have one left over.

$54 \div 6 = ?$
$9 \times 6 = 54$
So $54 \div 6 = 9$ bunches

Everything's quicker if you know your tables...

Learn your tables — it makes loads of Maths much easier. And remember, always <u>read</u> <u>questions</u> carefully. If you do the wrong calculation, you'll <u>definitely</u> get the wrong answer.

Square Numbers

Square Numbers

When you multiply a number by itself, you get a <u>SQUARE NUMBER</u>.
Here are the first 12 square numbers:

1	4	9	16	25	36	49	64	81	100	121	144...
(1×1)	(2×2)	(3×3)	(4×4)	(5×5)	(6×6)	(7×7)	(8×8)	(9×9)	(10×10)	(11×11)	(12×12)...

They're called <u>square numbers</u> because they are the areas in this pattern of squares.

$1 \times 1 = 1$

$2 \times 2 = 4$

$3 \times 3 = 9$

$4 \times 4 = 16$

There's a quick way to write them.
You write <u>five squared</u> as 5^2.

EXAMPLES:
a) $7^2 = 7$ squared $= 7 \times 7 = 49$.
b) $15^2 = 15$ squared $= 15 \times 15 = 225$.

Work hard to get ahead.

But I've already got a head.

EXAMPLE:

What is 40^2?

$$40^2 = \quad 40 \quad \times \quad 40$$
$$= 4 \times 10 \times 4 \times 10$$
$$= 4 \times 4 \times 10 \times 10$$
$$= 16 \times 100$$
$$= \underline{1600}$$

BE CAREFUL!
It's <u>NOT</u> $4^2 \times 10$

See page 22 for help with multiplying by 10 or 100.

Another Example

Find two different square numbers that add to 50.

Write down square numbers up to 50:   1   4   9   16   25   36   49

It's easy to see that to make 50, you just need to add 1 to 49.

$$1 + 49 = 50$$

Learning Objective:

"I can say the squares of numbers to 12×12 and work out the squares of multiples of 10."

Square Numbers

Question 1

Show that 10 is **not** a square number.
You may draw diagrams as part of your answer.

1 Think of a square number that's <u>close to 10</u>.
<u>9</u> is a square number.
Show this using a pattern of squares.

2 Now show that you <u>can't</u> arrange <u>10</u> small squares to form a square.

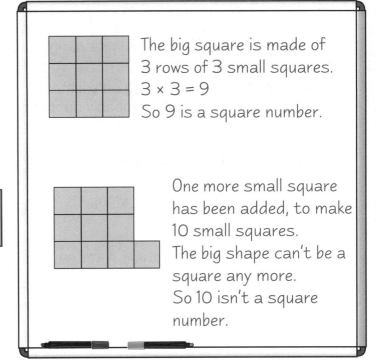

The big square is made of 3 rows of 3 small squares.
$3 \times 3 = 9$
So 9 is a square number.

One more small square has been added, to make 10 small squares.
The big shape can't be a square any more.
So 10 isn't a square number.

Question 2

What is 50^2?

1 Write out 50^2 <u>in full</u>.
Remember it's <u>NOT</u> $5^2 \times 10$.

2 50 is a <u>multiple of 10</u>, so you can <u>break the calculation down</u> into numbers that are easy to multiply.

3 Remember, you can <u>multiply</u> in <u>any order</u>. Rearrange the multiplication so that all the zeros are at the end. Then multiply in easy steps.

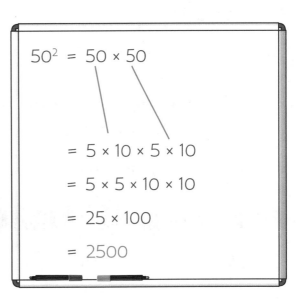

$50^2 = 50 \times 50$

$= 5 \times 10 \times 5 \times 10$

$= 5 \times 5 \times 10 \times 10$

$= 25 \times 100$

$= 2500$

Something squared = something × itself

It's good to learn all the square numbers up to 12^2. But if you forget, working them out is easy. Just <u>multiply the number by itself</u>. So 5^2 means 5×5, which is <u>25</u>. Job done.

Practice Questions

1   Kylie and Jason both work out the answer to 960 − 731.
     Kylie's answer is 239. Jason's answer is 229.

     Check both their answers by doing the inverse operation.
     Whose answer is correct?

2   Mildred works out that 59 × 11 = 6490.

     Check her answer by doing an estimate.
     Write down if Mildred is probably right or probably wrong.

3   Damian works out that 9 cm + 5 cm = 14 m.

     Explain why his answer is wrong.

4   One number is in the wrong place on the diagram below.

     Which number is in the wrong place?
     Explain your answer.

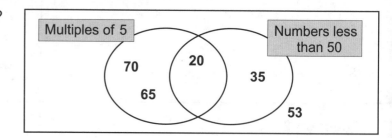

5   Here are 4 digit cards.

     5   2   1   6

     Choose two digit cards to make

     a)   a two-digit factor of 60.

     b)   a two-digit multiple of 8.

6   Which of these numbers are multiples of 2 **and** 9?

     18   27   32   54   12   72

7   Jessica is thinking of a 2-digit number.
     The number has 3 tens and is a multiple of 3 and 11.

     What number is Jessica thinking of?

Practice Questions

8   What are the missing numbers in these number sentences?

a) $8 \times 9 = \boxed{}$ b) $4 \times \boxed{} = 32$ c) $\boxed{} \times 9 = 54$

9   Sarah is organising a trip. She has booked 5 minibuses. Each minibus seats 9 people.

How many people can go on Sarah's trip?

10   Stephanie sells her chocolates in boxes of 9.

   a)   One day she makes 108 chocolates.
        How many boxes of chocolates can she make?

   b)   The next day she makes enough chocolates to fill 6 boxes exactly.
        How many chocolates does she make on this day?

11   Jeremy sells his jam tarts in packs of 8. He has 64 jam tarts.

How many packs of jam tarts can he make altogether?

12   Daphne is making necklaces. Each necklace uses 7 large beads.

Daphne has 60 large beads. How many necklaces can she make altogether?

13   James says, "36 is a square number."

Is James right? Draw a diagram to explain your answer.

14   Amy has 4^2 stickers. Ellen has 7^2 stickers.

How many more stickers does Ellen have than Amy?

15   What is 60^2?

16   Jade works in a book shop. She is packing an order of 80^2 Maths books.

How many Maths books does Jade need to pack?

Multiply and Divide by 10 and 100

× by 10 or 100 — Move the Digits to the Left

To <u>multiply by ten</u>, just <u>move</u> all the digits <u>one place value column</u> to the <u>left</u>. For example, 32 × 10 = 320. The number gets <u>ten times bigger</u>.

T U   H T U
3 2 × 1 0 = 3 2 0

You need this zero to fill the units place. It's called a <u>placeholder</u>.

The <u>2</u> moves from <u>units</u> to <u>tens</u>.
The <u>3</u> moves from <u>tens</u> to <u>hundreds</u>.

To <u>multiply by a hundred</u> just <u>move two places</u> to the left.

T U   Th H T U
6 4 × 1 0 0 = 6 4 0 0

Your number gets <u>100 times bigger</u>. You need <u>2 zeros</u> as placeholders.

÷ by 10 or 100 — Move the Digits to the Right

To divide by 10, move all the digits <u>1 place value column</u> to the <u>right</u>. The number gets <u>10 times smaller</u>.

H T U   T u . t
1 6 0 ÷ 1 0 = 1 6 . 0 = 1 6

16.0 = 16 so you don't need to write this zero.

To divide by 100, move everything <u>2 places</u> to the right. The number gets <u>100 times smaller</u>.

Th H T U   T u . t h
7 0 0 0 ÷ 1 0 0 = 7 0 . 0 0 = 7 0

You Might Get a Decimal Answer

Sometimes when you <u>divide</u> by 10 or 100 you <u>do</u> get a <u>decimal answer</u>.

EXAMPLE: Divide <u>728 by 10</u>.
Move all the digits <u>1 place value column</u> to the <u>right</u>.

You have to keep this, as it's not '0'.

H T U   T u . t
7 2 8 ÷ 1 0 = 7 2 . 8

Learning Objective:

"I can multiply and divide numbers by 10 or 100 and describe what happens to the digits."

Multiply and Divide by 10 and 100

Question 1

a)   Divide 764 by 10.
b)   How many hundreds are there in 8600?

a) ① Write down the calculation you need to do in <u>numbers</u>.

② Move the digits <u>one place</u> to the <u>right</u>.

b) ① Write down the calculation you need to do in <u>numbers</u>.

② Move all the digits <u>two places</u> to the <u>right</u>. You get **86.00** — but you don't need to write the zeros <u>after the decimal point</u>.

$$764 \div 10$$

$$\begin{array}{ll} \text{HTU} & \text{HTU.t} \\ 764 \div 10 = & 76.4 \end{array}$$

$$8600 \div 100$$

$$\begin{array}{ll} \text{ThH T U} & \text{ThH T U.t h} \\ 8600 \div 100 = & 86.00 = 86 \end{array}$$

Question 2

Jonathon thinks of a number. He divides the number by 100.
The answer he gets is **460**. What number was he thinking of?

① From the question you know that a number divided by 100 (made <u>100 times smaller</u>) is **460**.

② So the number you're looking for must be <u>100 times bigger</u> than **460**.

③ <u>Check your answer</u>. Divide by 100 as Jonathon does.

④ You get the <u>same answer</u> as Jonathon, so **46 000** must be right.

$$? \div 100 = 460$$

$$? \text{ must be } 460 \times 100 = 46\,000$$

$$46\,000 \div 100 = 460$$

Jonathon's number was 46 000.

Multiply by 10 — the number gets 10 times bigger...

To <u>multiply</u> by 10 or 100 you move the digits to the <u>left</u> and add zeros as placeholders.
To <u>divide</u> by 10 or 100 you move the digits to the <u>right</u> and some zeros might disappear.

Mental Maths

Add and Subtract in Two Stages...

EXAMPLE: What is 37 + 52?

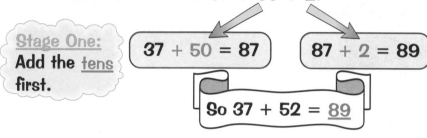

Keep 37 as it is and partition 52.

37 + 52 is the same as 37 + 50 + 2."

Stage One: Add the tens first.

37 + 50 = 87   87 + 2 = 89

Stage Two: Add the units to the answer.

So 37 + 52 = 89

You can subtract by partitioning too...

> **EXAMPLE:** What is 63 – 22? Partition 22 into 20 and 2.
>
> 63 – 20 = 43, 43 – 2 = 41... so 63 – 22 = 41

...Or Make an Easier Sum First

A good way is to use a near, easy number and then adjust your answer.

EXAMPLE: What is 16 + 29?

Instead of adding 29, you would add 30 then subtract 1 (because you've added 1 too many).

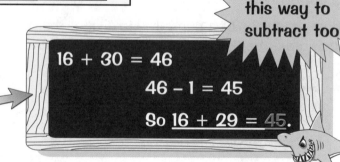

You can use this way to subtract too.

16 + 30 = 46

46 – 1 = 45

So 16 + 29 = 45.

Subtract by Counting On to the Bigger Number

Sometimes it's quicker to subtract by counting on. You need to imagine a number line in your head. You start at the smaller number and count on in easy steps.

Here is 92 – 83 with this method.

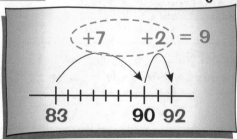

+7   +2 = 9

83   90 92

Learning Objective:

"I can use mental addition and subtraction to help me solve problems."

Mental Maths

Question 1

What is the **difference** between **87** and **39**? Work it out in your head.

① You need to <u>subtract 39</u> from **87**.

② Think of an <u>easier calculation</u> you can do. You can <u>subtract 40</u> and then <u>adjust</u> by <u>adding 1</u>.

③ Do the calculations.

④ <u>Check</u> your answer.

$87 - 39$

$87 - 40 + 1$

$87 - 40 = 47$
$47 + 1 = 48$

$48 + 39 = 70 + 9 + 8 = 87$
So 48 is the correct answer.

Question 2

Kelly is **17**. Her Dad says, "To work out my age, **double** Kelly's age and then **add 27**."
How old is **Kelly's Dad**? Work it out in your head.

① Work out the calculation you need to do in <u>numbers</u>.

② Work out <u>double 17</u>. You can <u>partition</u> to make this easier.

③ Now <u>add 27</u> to **34**. Add 20 first, then 7.

④ Write down the <u>final answer</u>.

$17 \times 2 + 27$

$17 = 10 + 7$
Double 10 = 20
Double 7 = 14
20 + 14 = 34

$27 = 20 + 7$
34 + 20 = 54
54 + 7 = 61

Kelly's Dad is 61 years old.

Partition by splitting into tens and units...

There's no need to panic about mental maths. The best thing to do is to <u>practise</u> all the easy ways to do things, like <u>partitioning</u> or doing an <u>easier calculation</u> and <u>adjusting</u>.

Written Adding and Subtracting

You Can Add In Columns

EXAMPLE: Work out 681 + 556 without using a calculator.

1 Arrange the numbers into their place value columns.

```
Th H T U
   6 8 1
 +   5 5 6
```

2 Add the units column first.

(It's the place value column of least value.)

```
Th H T U
   6 8 1
 +   5 5 6
         7        1 + 6 = 7
```

3 Add the tens column next...

8 + 5 = 13
The 3 goes in the tens answer space...

```
Th H T U
   6 8 1
 +   5 5 6
        3 7
         1
```

10 tens = 100.
So put 100 below the hundreds column.

4 ...then the hundreds.

6 + 5 + 1 = 12

2 goes in the hundreds column...

10 hundreds = 1000.
So put 1000 in the thousands answer space.

```
Th H T U
   6 8 1
 +   5 5 6
   1 2 3 7
     1
```

So...
681 + 556
= 1237

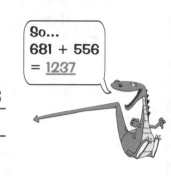

You Can Add Decimals in the Same Way

EXAMPLE: Work out 23.83 + 35.4

When you write the numbers down, always line up the decimal points.
Then start adding, beginning with the place value column of least value (it's always on the right).

1 Add the hundredths.

Always put the decimal point in first.

```
T U t h
2 3.8 3
+ 3 5.4 0
      . 3
```

You can put in a zero here, to show there are no hundredths.
3 + 0 = 3

2 Add the tenths.

10 tenths = 1.
So put the 1 below the units column.

```
T U t h
2 3.8 3
+ 3 5.4 0
    . 2 3
        1
```

8 + 4 = 12

3 Add the units.

3 + 5 + 1 = 9

Remember to add this 1 too.

```
T U t h
2 3.8 3
+ 3 5.4 0
  9.2 3
      1
```

4 Add the tens.

To finish, add up the last column.
2 + 3 = 5

```
T U t h
2 3.8 3
+ 3 5.4 0
5 9.2 3
      1
```

So 23.83 +
35.4 = 59.23
(Don't forget the decimal point.)

Learning Objective:

"I can use standard written methods to add whole numbers and decimals."

Written Adding and Subtracting

Question 1

Calculate **269 + 29 + 507**.

1 Line up the units, tens and hundreds.
Start with the column of least place value —
add the units. **9 + 9 + 7 = 25**
Put the 2 tens under the tens column.

```
    269
  +  29
  + 507
      5
     2
```

2 Add the tens column. Remember to
include the 2 tens at the bottom.
6 tens + 2 tens + 2 tens = 10 tens.
10 tens = 100, so write 0 in the tens
answer space and 1 hundred under
the hundreds column.

```
    269
  +  29
  + 507
     05
    1 2
```

3 Finally add the hundreds column.
**2 hundreds + 5 hundreds + 1 hundred
= 8 hundreds.**

```
    269
  +  29
  + 507
    805          269 + 29 + 507 = 805
    1 2
```

Question 2

A shop sells 3 types of lipstick for **£1.99**, **£3.49** and **£5.79**. Anna buys one of the cheapest lipsticks and one of the most expensive ones. How much does Anna spend altogether?

1 Write down the calculation in columns,
lining up the decimal points.
Write a decimal point in the answer space.

Start by adding the hundredths.
9 hundredths + 9 hundredths = 18 hundredths.

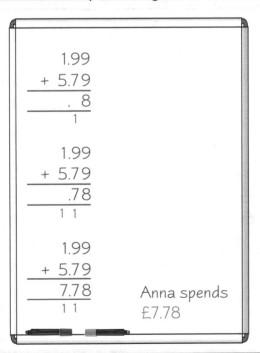

```
   1.99
 + 5.79
   . 8
   1
```

2 Add the tenths.
9 tenths + 7 tenths + 1 tenth = 17 tenths.

```
   1.99
 + 5.79
   .78
   1 1
```

3 Finally add the units. **1 + 5 + 1 = 7**

4 Write the answer in pounds and pence.

```
   1.99
 + 5.79
   7.78         Anna spends
   1 1          £7.78
```

Start adding with the column on the right...

It's important to line up the columns properly before you start adding. With decimals, the decimal points should all be in line. And remember to put a decimal point in the answer.

Written Adding and Subtracting

In Subtractions, You May Need to Exchange

You set out <u>subtractions</u> the same way as additions. Line up the <u>units</u> or decimal points. Then you start subtracting with the column of <u>least place value</u>.

EXAMPLE: What is <u>835 – 296</u>?

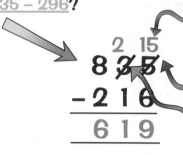

$$\begin{array}{r} {}^{2}\;{}^{15} \\ 8\,\cancel{3}\,\cancel{5} \\ -\,2\,1\,6 \\ \hline 6\,1\,9 \end{array}$$

1) You can't do 5 – 6 because 6 is bigger than 5.

2) But you can <u>exchange</u> a <u>ten</u> from the 30 for <u>10 units</u>. Add those 10 units onto the 5 to make 15. Then 15 – 6 = <u>9</u>.

3) There's <u>10 less</u> here because you changed a ten into units.

Subtracting in Columns

EXAMPLE: Work out <u>83 – 9.6</u> without using a calculator.

① Line up the decimal points.

$$\begin{array}{r} T\;\;U.t \\ 8\;3.0 \\ -\;\;\;9.6 \\ \hline . \end{array}$$

<u>83</u> means <u>83.0</u>

② <u>Subtract the TENTHS.</u> You can't do 0 – 6, so exchange one of the <u>units</u> for 10 tenths. Then 10 – 6 = 4.

$$\begin{array}{r} T\;\;U.t \\ {}^{2}{}^{1} \\ 8\;\cancel{3}.0 \\ -\;\;\;9.6 \\ \hline .4 \end{array}$$

③ <u>Subtract the UNITS.</u> You can't do 2 – 9, so exchange a <u>ten</u> for 10 units. Then 12 – 9 = 3.

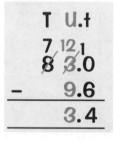

$$\begin{array}{r} T\;\;U.t \\ {}^{7}\;{}^{12}{}^{1} \\ \cancel{8}\;\cancel{3}.0 \\ -\;\;\;9.6 \\ \hline 3.4 \end{array}$$

④ <u>Subtract the TENS.</u> 7 – 0 = 7

$$\begin{array}{r} T\;\;U.t \\ {}^{7}\;{}^{12}{}^{1} \\ \cancel{8}\;\cancel{3}.0 \\ -\;\;\;9.6 \\ \hline 7\,3.4 \end{array}$$

You Can Exchange Across Several Columns

Subtracting from a number with <u>zeros</u> in is a bit harder.

$$\begin{array}{r} 2\;0\;3 \\ -\,1\,1\,6 \\ \hline \end{array}$$

You can't do 3 – 6. But there are <u>no tens</u> to exchange for 10 units...

...so you'll have to exchange a <u>hundred</u> for <u>10 tens</u>.

Then exchange a <u>ten</u> for <u>10 units</u>. So you have <u>9 tens</u> left.

Now you have 13 units so you can subtract. 13 – 6 = 7

$$\begin{array}{r} {}^{9} \\ {}^{10}{}^{1} \\ {}^{1}\cancel{2}\;\cancel{0}\;3 \\ -\,1\,1\,6 \\ \hline 8\,7 \end{array}$$

1 – 1 = 0   9 – 1 = 8

Learning Objective:

"I can use standard written methods to subtract whole numbers and decimals."

Written Adding and Subtracting

Question 1

Calculate **843 – 327**.

1 Write down the numbers in columns, lining up units, tens and hundreds. Start by subtracting the units. 3 – 7 doesn't work, so exchange 1 ten for 10 units. Now you can do 13 – 7 = 6.

$$\begin{array}{r} 8\overset{3}{4}\overset{1}{3} \\ -\ 327 \\ \hline 6 \end{array}$$

2 Now subtract the tens. 3 tens – 2 tens = 1 ten

$$\begin{array}{r} 8\overset{3}{4}\overset{1}{3} \\ -\ 327 \\ \hline 16 \end{array}$$

3 Finally subtract the hundreds. 8 hundreds – 3 hundreds = 5 hundreds

$$\begin{array}{r} 8\overset{3}{4}\overset{1}{3} \\ -\ 327 \\ \hline 516 \end{array}$$

Question 2

Katie has **£5.52**. For lunch she buys a pizza that costs **£3.69**.
Does Katie have enough money left to buy a magazine that costs **£1.99**? Show your method.

1 Work out what calculation you need to do.

You have to work out £5.52 – £3.69, to see if it's £1.99 or more.

2 Subtract the hundredths first. 2 – 9 doesn't work so exchange 1 tenth for 10 hundredths. Now you have 12 hundredths.

$$\begin{array}{r} 5.5\overset{4}{\cancel{2}}^{1} \\ -\ 3.69 \\ \hline .\ 3 \end{array}$$

12 hundredths – 9 hundredths = 3 hundredths

3 Subtract the tenths. 4 – 6 doesn't work, so exchange 1 unit for 10 tenths. Now, 14 tenths – 6 tenths = 8 tenths

$$\begin{array}{r} {}^{4}\cancel{5}.{}^{14}\cancel{5}{}^{1}2 \\ -\ 3.69 \\ \hline .83 \end{array}$$

4 Finally subtract the units. 4 – 3 = 1

5 Remember to include the unit. In this case it's pounds.

$$\begin{array}{r} {}^{4}\cancel{5}.{}^{14}\cancel{5}{}^{1}2 \\ -\ 3.69 \\ \hline 1.83 \end{array}$$

Katie only has £1.83 left so she can't buy the magazine.

When you subtract in columns, you can exchange...

Exchanging is really important. You can't subtract a bigger number from a smaller number. So you might need to exchange a ten for 10 units, or a hundred for 10 tens, and so on.

Written Multiplying and Dividing

You Can Multiply in Columns

EXAMPLE: What is 124 × 8?

Arrange the numbers in place value columns.
Then multiply the 8 by the units, tens and hundreds.

①
```
H T U
1 2 4
×   8
    2
3
```
8 × 4 = 32. Write the 2 in the units answer space and the 3 tens below the tens column.

②
```
H T U
1 2 4
×   8
  9 2
1 3
```
8 × 20 = 160. Add on the 3 tens to make 190. Write down the 9 tens and put the 1 hundred below the hundreds column.

③
```
H T U
1 2 4
×   8
9 9 2
1 3
```
8 × 100 = 800. Add on the 1 hundred to make 900.

HARDER EXAMPLE: What is 26 × 42?

STAGE 1: 2 × 26

2 × 6 = 12 Write down the 2 and put the 1 ten in the tens column.

2 × 20 = 40 so add 40 to the other 10 = 50. So the first row is 52.

```
  2 6
×  4 2
  5 2
  1
1 0 4 0
  2
1 0 9 2
```

STAGE 2: 40 × 26

40 × 6 = 240
Write down the 40 and put the 200 below the hundreds column.

40 × 20 = 800. Add this 800 to the 200. That makes 1000. So the second row is 1040.

STAGE 3: Add up the two rows.

Multiplying Decimals

To multiply decimals, do a whole number calculation, then adjust.

EXAMPLE:
What is 2.3 × 5?

To get a whole number calculation, multiply 2.3 by 10 to get 23.
Do the calculation with this whole number: 23 × 5 = 115.
Now adjust the answer. You have to divide by 10: 115 ÷ 10 = 11.5

Divide by Subtracting Multiples

EXAMPLE: What is 159 divided by 5?

Find a multiple of 5 that is just below 159.
E.g. 5 × 30 = 150. Subtract this multiple.

The largest multiple of 5 you can subtract now is 5.

```
5 | 1 5 9
  - 1 5 0      ← 5 × 30 = 150
      9
  -   5      ← 5 × 1 = 5
      4            31
```

Add together all the multiples.

5 can't go into 4. So the answer is 31 r 4.

Learning Objective:

"I can use standard written methods to multiply and divide whole numbers and decimals."

Written Multiplying and Dividing

Question 1

There are **28** rulers in a box. A school buys **33** boxes of rulers.
Will the school have enough new rulers for its **900** pupils?

1 Write 28 × 33 in columns.
Then the first step is to work out <u>28 × 3</u>.

2 The second step is 28 × 30.

3 <u>Add up</u> the two rows to find the total number of rulers.
And remember to <u>answer the question</u>.

$$\begin{array}{r} 28 \\ \times\ 33 \\ \hline 84 \\ {\scriptstyle 2} \end{array}$$
  8 × 3 = 24
  20 × 3 = 60

$$\begin{array}{r} 28 \\ \times\ 33 \\ \hline 84 \\ {\scriptstyle 2} \\ 840 \\ {\scriptstyle 2} \end{array}$$
  8 × 30 = 240
  20 × 30 = 600

$$\begin{array}{r} 28 \\ \times\ 33 \\ \hline 84 \\ {\scriptstyle 2} \\ 840 \\ {\scriptstyle 2} \\ \hline 924 \\ {\scriptstyle 1} \end{array}$$

There are 924 rulers in total so the school does have enough for all its pupils.

Question 2

157 pupils must be organised into **6** school teams, with the same number of pupils in each team.
How many pupils will be in **each team**? Will there be any pupils **left over**?

1 Write down the calculation. It's 157 ÷ 6.

2 Find a <u>multiple of 6</u> that is <u>just below 157</u>.

3 <u>Subtract</u> this multiple from 157.

4 You've got 37 left. Subtract the largest multiple of 6 you can, which is <u>36</u>.

5 6 can't go into 1 so your answer is <u>26 r 1</u>.
<u>Answer the question</u> by writing a sentence.

$6\overline{)157}$

Try 6 × 10 = 60. Not very close.
Try 6 × 20 = <u>120</u>. Close enough.

$$\begin{array}{r} 6\overline{)157} \\ -\ 120 \\ \hline 37 \\ -\ 36 \\ \hline 1 \end{array}$$
  → 6 × 20 = 120
  → 6 × 6 = 36
  26

There will be 26 pupils in each team, with 1 pupil left over.

Partitioning can make multiplying easier...

When you're multiplying two-digit numbers, remember you can always partition the numbers to make the multiplications easier. So, 7 × 32 becomes 7 × 30 add 7 × 2.

Calculators

The Four Golden Rules

1) Make sure it says '0' <u>before you start</u>.
2) Press the buttons <u>carefully</u>.
3) <u>Always check the display</u> to make sure you've pressed the right button.
4) Press the ⊟ button <u>at the end</u> of every calculation.

If You Press the Wrong Button...

Press the [C] button (or [CE] or [DEL] button on some calculators).
This will cancel the number you just typed in. Then you can carry on.

Make Sure You Use the Same Units

EXAMPLE: Tasha buys some sweets costing 92p, some apples costing £2.42 and a drink costing 76p. How much change will she get from £10.00?

First convert 92p and 76p into <u>pounds</u>. 92p = £0.92   76p = £0.76

Then <u>subtract</u> all the numbers from £10.00 ← Just put "10" into your calculator — you don't need the decimal places.

$$1\ 0\ -\ 0\ .\ 9\ 2\ -\ 2\ .\ 4\ 2\ -\ 0\ .\ 7\ 6\ =$$

The display will read: | 5.9 | So the answer is <u>£5.90</u>. ← Don't forget the units — you've been working in pounds.

Recognising Negative Numbers...

EXAMPLE: A part of Darshna's bank statement looks like this. How much money does Darshna have in her account?

205.85
+ 25.93
− 602.02
+ 70.25

Do this calculation using your calculator:
205.85 + 25.93 − 602.02 + 70.25

The display will read: | −299.99 | So Darshna has <u>−£299.99</u> in her bank account.

(The minus sign means that Darshna owes the bank £299.99.)

Learning Objective:

"I can use a calculator to solve problems."

Calculators

Question 1

 A packet of balloons costs **£1.59**. Lucy buys **8 packets** of balloons. How much **change** will she get from **£20**?

1 Work out how much money Lucy has spent altogether. <u>Multiply</u> **£1.59 × 8.**

2 Now subtract this amount from **£20.**

3 Remember to write your answer in <u>pounds</u> and <u>pence</u>.

1.59 × 8 = 12.72 = £12.72

20 – 12.72 = 7.28

Lucy will get £7.28 change.

Question 2

 Emma has **£34.05** in her bank account. She is given **£20** for her birthday and puts this in the bank. She spends **£4.95** on a new diary and **£55** on a bag. **How much** money will Emma have in her bank account now?

1 Emma has £34.05 to start with. You have to <u>add £20</u>, then <u>subtract £4.95</u>, then <u>subtract £55</u>.

2 Work it out on your <u>calculator</u>. Remember to write the number on the display in <u>pounds and pence</u>.

3 A <u>negative number</u> means that Emma <u>doesn't have enough money</u> in her bank account — she owes the bank £5.90.

34.05 + 20 – 4.95 – 55

= –5.9 = –£5.90

Emma has –£5.90 in her bank account.

Make sure you know what the buttons do...

Don't worry if you make a mistake typing numbers into your calculator. You don't have to start all over again... as long you know <u>which button</u> to press to delete the last entry.

Practice Questions

1   There are 42 monkeys at the zoo. Each monkey eats 10 bananas.

How many bananas do the monkeys eat in total?

2   Jim has a sheet of 220 stickers. He gives 10 to each of his friends.

He has no stickers left.
How many people did he give stickers to?

3   Zoë is stuck in a traffic jam. There are 22 lorries and 56 cars in front of her.

How many vehicles are in front of Zoë in the traffic jam? Work it out in your head.

4   150 people went to the school disco.

69 were boys. How many were girls? Work it out in your head.

5   7643 people went to a football match in Manchester.
6391 people went to a football match in Glasgow.

How many people went to these two football matches altogether?

6   Grace went shopping. Below are three of her receipts.

Receipt 1   Receipt 2   Receipt 3

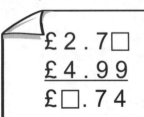

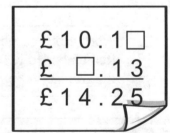

a)   Work out the missing numbers in her receipts.

b)   How much did she spend in total?

7   Louise has 238 sweets. Her friends eat 154 of them.

How many sweets are left?

Practice Questions

8   Henry gets £16.25 for his birthday.

He gives £2.68 to his sister. How much money does Henry have left?

9   Dave buys a shirt for £9.79 and a CD for £3.49

How much change will he get from £20?

10   Nadia and three friends see this notice.

Nadia donates £32.50 to the charity.
Her friends donate £127 each.
How much more money will the charity still need?

> **Please help** us to save the
> Cumbrian Hairy Toad!
> We still need to raise £1583!

11   James buys 3 boxes of jelly beans. There are 16 flavours of jelly bean.
Each box has 25 jelly beans of each flavour.

a)   How many jelly beans are there in one box?

b)   How many jelly beans has James bought in total?

12   Simon buys 163 flowers. He wants to split the flowers into 7 equal bunches.

a)   How many flowers will be in each bunch?

b)   How many flowers will be left over?

13   Sophie buys 6 drinks costing 60p each and 4 cakes costing £1.20 each.

How much does she pay altogether?

14   Pairs of socks cost £2.99 and hats cost £5.89. Chloe buys 3 pairs of socks and 2 hats.

 How much change will she get from £25?

2D Shapes

Polygons *have* Straight Sides

The <u>name</u> of a polygon tells you <u>how many sides and angles</u> it has.

<u>tri</u>angle	<u>quad</u>rilateral	<u>pent</u>agon	<u>hex</u>agon	<u>hept</u>agon	<u>oct</u>agon
3 sides	4 sides	5 sides	6 sides	7 sides	8 sides
3 angles	4 angles	5 angles	6 angles	7 angles	8 angles

Regular *Polygons have* Equal Length Sides

<u>Regular polygons</u> have <u>equal length sides</u> and <u>equal angles</u>.
<u>Irregular polygons</u> have at least one <u>side</u> or <u>angle</u> that's <u>different</u>.

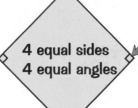

4 equal sides
4 equal angles

Each angle is a right angle (90°). It's just a quarter of a turn.

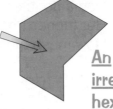

2 pairs of equal sides

An <u>irregular</u> <u>hex</u>agon

<u>Squares</u> are regular polygons.

<u>Rectangles</u> are irregular polygons.

There are Different *Types of* Triangle

AN EQUILATERAL TRIANGLE

3 equal sides
3 equal angles

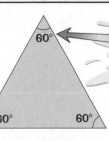

Each angle in an equilateral triangle is 60°.

A RIGHT-ANGLED TRIANGLE
1 angle is a <u>right angle</u>.

AN ISOSCELES TRIANGLE

2 equal sides
2 equal angles

A SCALENE TRIANGLE
<u>All</u> the sides and angles are <u>different</u>.

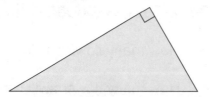

Learning Objective:

"I can name polygons. I can say whether a triangle is equilateral, isosceles or scalene and explain how I know."

2D Shapes

Question 1

Use this grid of dots to draw
a)   an **isosceles** triangle — label it **I**.
b)   a **scalene** triangle — label it **S**.

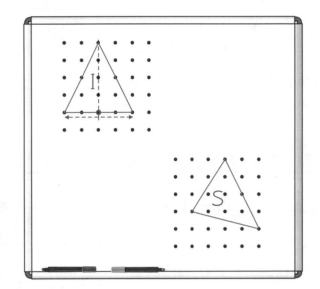

a An isosceles triangle has two sides the same length, so it's symmetrical.

b All three sides of a scalene triangle are different lengths. Measure the sides of your triangle to make sure.

Question 2

Here are six shapes.
One of them is a **regular heptagon**.
Put a tick (✓) in the regular heptagon.

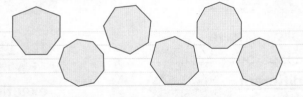

1 A heptagon has seven sides. So start by counting the sides of each shape. Three of the shapes are heptagons.

2 The regular heptagon is the one with sides that are all the same length.

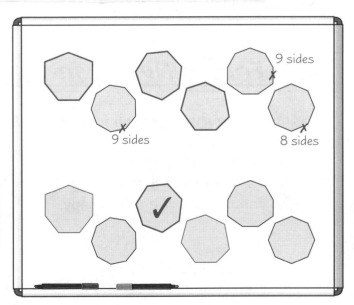

9 sides

9 sides

8 sides

✓

Learn the names of common shapes...

There are lots of words to learn for the topic of shapes. Most 2D shapes have names ending in "-agon" though — so you just have to learn the bit in front.

3D Shapes

The Name Tells You the Number of Faces

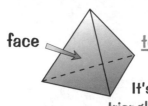

face

tetrahedron
4 faces

It's also called a
triangle-based pyramid.

octahedron
8 faces

hexahedron
6 faces
A cube is a regular
hexahedron.

Regular 3D shapes have regular polygon faces. For example, regular tetrahedron and octahedron faces are all equilateral triangles. Regular hexahedron faces are squares.

Some Special 3D Shapes you Need to Know...

Some are cuboids (boxes)...

Cubes and cuboids always have **6 faces** and **8 vertices**.

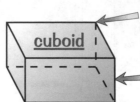

cuboid

vertex (just a fancy word for corner)

edge

Corners are called vertices ("verti-sees").

Some are pyramids...

Pyramids always have triangular sides but can have **different shaped bases**.

And some are prisms...

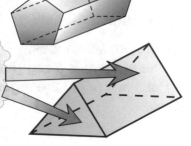

The two end faces of a prism are exactly the same.

You Fold a Net to make a 3D Shape

Look at the shape of each face on a 3D solid. These shapes must be part of the solid's net.
There's often more than one net you can use to make a 3D shape.

EXAMPLE:

A cube has 6 square faces...
So its net needs 6 squares...

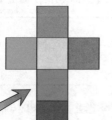

An open cube is a cube with one face missing.

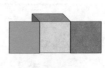

So the net only has 5 squares.

Learning Objective:

"I can use the properties of 3D shapes to draw their nets accurately."

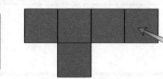

3D Shapes

Question 1

Look at these diagrams.
Two of the diagrams are nets for a regular **octahedron**.
Put ticks (✓) in them.

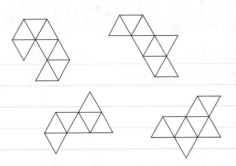

① **Count** the <u>triangles</u> in each diagram. An octahedron has <u>8 faces</u>. The diagram in the bottom left only has <u>7</u> triangles. So that can't be one.

② Now imagine <u>folding</u> the nets together.

③ If you tried to fold up the first one, the red faces would <u>overlap</u>.

④ So the two that are left must be right.

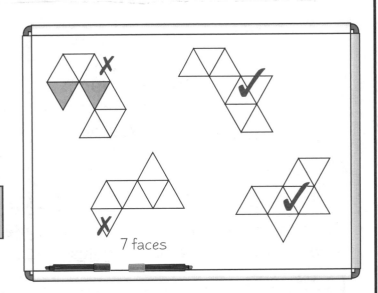

7 faces

Question 2

This diagram shows a cube. **Draw** a **net** for the cube.
Then colour your net so that **opposite faces** on the cube are the **same colour**.

① First you need to <u>draw</u> a <u>net</u> for a cube. The net must have <u>6 square faces</u>.

② <u>Colour in</u> one of the faces, e.g. green. Imagine <u>folding</u> the net together, so you can tell which side is <u>opposite</u> the green side. Colour this side green too.

③ <u>Repeat</u> this with <u>two other colours</u>. You should end up with 3 sets of 2 faces, each a different colour. <u>Check</u> that your net is correct by imagining it folded up.

If imagining a shape is hard, try making a model...

Nets can be tricky things to do in your head. If you're really struggling with a nets question, try actually making the shape. Then you might find it easier to imagine next time.

Angles

Angles *Measure* How Far *Something* Turns

Angles tell you <u>how far something has turned</u>. The bigger the angle, the bigger the turn.
Angles are measured in <u>degrees</u> (°).

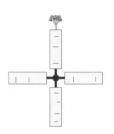

A <u>quarter</u> turn is
<u>90</u> degrees (90°).
A quarter turn is also
called a <u>right angle</u>.

A <u>half</u> turn is
<u>180</u> degrees (180°).
It's the same as
2 right angles.

A <u>full</u> turn is
<u>360</u> degrees (360°).
It's the same as
4 right angles.

You Can Compare *Angles by* Size

An angle <u>smaller than 90°</u> is called an <u>acute</u> angle. An angle <u>bigger than 90°</u> but
<u>smaller than 180°</u> is called an <u>obtuse</u> angle. (You can use a <u>set square</u> to compare angles to 90°.)

EXAMPLE: Look at the angles below. Circle the <u>smallest angle</u>.
Tick the angle that is <u>bigger</u> than a right angle.

This angle is a
right angle.

These are both <u>acute</u> angles.

This is the smallest angle.

This is smaller than
a right angle but it's
not the smallest.

This is bigger
than a right
angle.
(It is <u>obtuse</u>.)

Use a Protractor (Angle Measurer) *to* Measure Angles

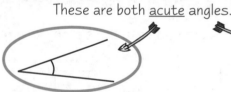

1 Put the <u>cross on the protractor</u> over the <u>vertex</u> of the angle.

2 <u>Line up</u> the <u>bottom line on the protractor</u> with one line of your angle.

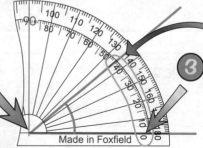
Made in Foxfield

3 Just <u>read</u> the scale. Use the scale that has <u>0</u> on the line of your angle.
This angle measures <u>45</u>°.

Learning Objective:

"I can estimate and measure the size of an
angle in degrees."

Angles

Question 1

Nathan is facing **north**. He turns **clockwise** until he is facing **west**.
How many degrees has he turned through?

1 Draw a <u>picture</u> to show Nathan's starting and finishing directions. Draw the <u>angle</u> between them.

2 Work out what <u>fraction</u> of a <u>full turn</u> the angle is.

3 Each <u>quarter</u> turn is 90°, so three quarters of a turn is three times 90°.

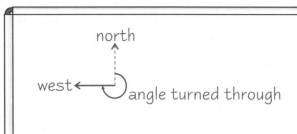

north

west ← angle turned through

Angle = ¾ of a turn

Angle = 3 × 90°
Angle = 270°

Question 2

Look at these six angles.

a) Which three angles are **acute**?
b) Which is the **largest** angle?
c) Which two angles are the **same size**?

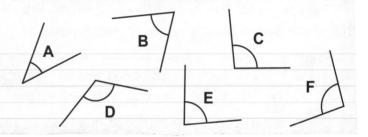

a <u>Acute</u> angles are <u>less</u> than 90°. You can tell just by looking that **A** and **B** are acute. The third acute angle is **E** — you could use a <u>set square</u> or <u>protractor</u> to check.

b Now look for the <u>largest</u> angle.

c There are three angles that <u>look similar</u> — **C**, **E** and **F**. <u>Measure</u> each one with a protractor (angle measurer).

a) A, B and E are acute angles

b) D is the largest angle

c) C and F are the same size

Remember — a right angle is 90°...

Protractors are really handy if you use them properly, but they can be a bit tricky to read. They have two scales, so always make sure you're reading the right one.

Coordinates

Go Across then Up to find the Position

Each point on a grid has two numbers to show its position.
These are called coordinates.

Coordinates tell you how many across and how many up from 0 a point is. You find them using the x-axis and y-axis.

The y-axis is a vertical line on the left of the grid.

The x-axis is a horizontal line across the bottom of the grid.

Gary

Coordinates are always put in brackets like this: (1, 4).

(0, 0) is called the origin.

EXAMPLE: Gary's coordinates are: **(3, 2)**

The x-coordinate tells you how many across.

The y-coordinate tells you how many up.

You always put the x-coordinate before the y-coordinate.
Here are some handy ways to remember it:

1) The two coordinates are in alphabetical order — x then y.
2) The x axis goes across the page.
   In other words "x is a..cross", get it? — x is a "✗".
3) You always go in the house (→) and then
   up the stairs (↑), so it's along first and then up.

You Can Work Out Coordinates

EXAMPLE:

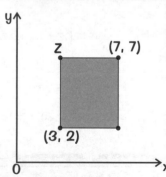

This is a shaded rectangle.
Find the coordinates of point Z.

Point Z is directly above the point at (3, 2).
So it must have the same x-coordinate, 3.
Point Z is straight across from the point at (7, 7).
So it must have the same y-coordinate, 7.

So Z's coordinates must be (3, 7).

Learning Objective:

"I can read and plot coordinates to make shapes."

Coordinates

Question 1

A, B and C are three vertices of a **rectangle**.
Write the coordinates of the fourth vertex.

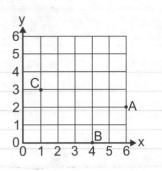

1. Draw in the two sides of the rectangle you're sure of.

2. Draw in lines parallel to the ones you've just drawn, starting from points A and C.

3. The fourth vertex is where they meet. Read its coordinates from the graph.

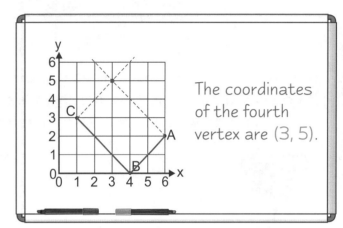

The coordinates of the fourth vertex are (3, 5).

Question 2

The diagram shows a **square** plotted on a set of axes.
Write the coordinates of point **A**.

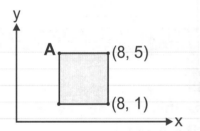

1. Point A is directly across from (8, 5), so its y-coordinate must be 5.

2. You know the shape is a square, so its width is the same as its height. You can work out its height as 4 units.

3. So the x-coordinate must be 4 units less than 8.

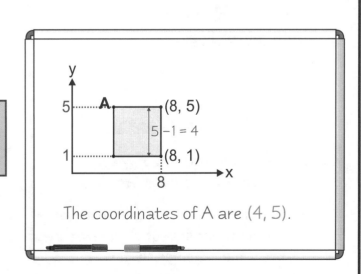

The coordinates of A are (4, 5).

Get your x and y coordinates the right way round...

The trickiest thing with coordinates is getting your x and y coordinates the right way round. There are a few ways to help you remember it — choose the one that works for you.

Symmetry

Some Shapes have Reflective Symmetry

This shape has a mirror line. It is also called the line of symmetry.
The two halves of the shape fit exactly one on top of each other.

Mirror line

Bob looks in the mirror.
It looks as if he can see
the whole shape.

If you can draw two mirror lines you say there are two lines of symmetry.
If you can draw three there are three lines of symmetry. And so on...
If you can't draw any mirror lines there are no lines of symmetry.

| 1 LINE OF SYMMETRY | 2 LINES OF SYMMETRY | 3 LINES OF SYMMETRY | NO LINES OF SYMMETRY | NO LINES OF SYMMETRY |

Reflecting Shapes in a Mirror Line

EXAMPLE:

Complete this drawing
so that the shape is
symmetrical about
both mirror lines.

Mirror
Line

Mirror Line

ANSWER:

Reflect the vertices one at a time:

1. Count the squares between
   the vertex and the mirror line.

2. Count the same number of squares
   on the other side of the mirror line.
   Draw the reflected vertex.

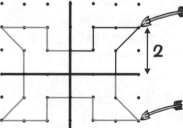

This vertex is 2 squares
from the horizontal
mirror line...

So the reflected
vertex must be 2
squares away too.

Learning Objective:

"I can draw a symmetrical shape."

Symmetry

Question 1

Complete this shape so that it is symmetrical in **both** mirror lines.

Use a ruler.

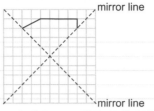

1. <u>Turn</u> the paper so that one mirror line is <u>vertical</u>. That makes it easier to count the grid squares either side.

2. Draw a <u>dot</u> where each reflected <u>vertex</u> will be. <u>Turn</u> the paper the other way so that the second mirror line is <u>vertical</u>. Draw <u>dots</u> to mark the vertices.

3. <u>Join</u> the dots with straight lines using a <u>ruler</u>.

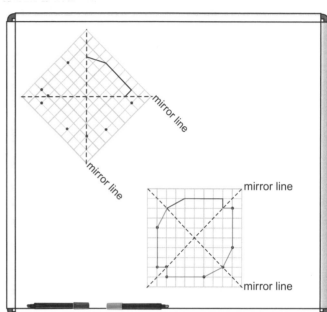

Question 2

Which of these shapes have **reflective symmetry**?

You may use a mirror or tracing paper.

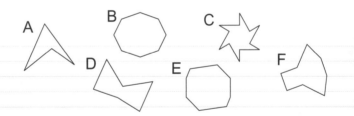

1. Look at <u>each shape</u> in turn and try to find a line of symmetry. You can use a mirror to help you.

2. Be careful. Some shapes, like E, look as though they could have a line of symmetry but <u>don't</u>.

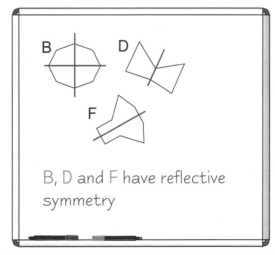

B, D and F have reflective symmetry

Regular shapes have at least one line of symmetry...

The most important thing with symmetry questions is to take your time.

If you're not sure about an answer, use a mirror or tracing paper to check.

Practice Questions

1   A shape has four straight sides.

What type of shape is it?

2   Which of these triangles are isosceles?

3   Imagine a prism whose end faces are hexagons.

a)   How many faces does it have?

b)   How many vertices does it have?

4   Write the names of the shapes that can be formed from these nets.

a)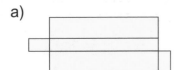

b)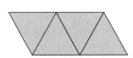

c)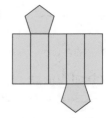

5   Draw a net for an open cube — a cube with no top.

6   Copy this diagram. Draw three more lines on it to make a hexagon that has two right angles.

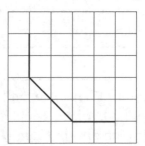

7   Look at this angle.

a)   Is it acute or obtuse?

b)   Measure it in degrees.

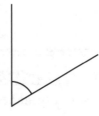

Practice Questions

8   This pattern is formed by rotating the shape 90° anticlockwise each time.

Copy the third shape. Shade it to continue the pattern.

9   A map has been drawn on this grid.

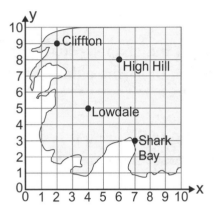

a)   Write the coordinates of Shark Bay.

b)   Write the coordinates of High Hill.

10   Two identical squares are drawn on this grid.

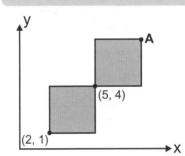

Penny says, "The coordinates of point A are (8, 6)."

Explain why she can't be right.

11   Copy this drawing onto dotted paper.
Complete the drawing so that it is
symmetrical in both mirror lines.

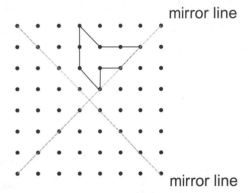

12   Which of these shapes have at least two lines of symmetry?

A   B   C   D   E

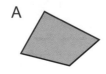   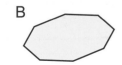   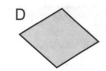

Calculating Perimeter and Area

Finding the Perimeter of a Shape

Perimeter is the distance all the way around the outside of a 2D (flat) shape.
To find the perimeter, you add up the lengths of all the sides.

1)   Put a cross at one vertex.

2)   Go around the shape, adding up the lengths of all the sides.

3)   Keep going until you get back to your cross, then stop.

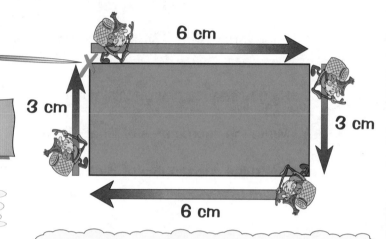

6 cm

3 cm

3 cm

6 cm

Perimeter = 6 + 3 + 6 + 3 = 18 cm

You Can Estimate Area by Counting Squares

You can find areas by counting how many squares or half-squares are covered on a grid. But not all shapes fit neatly into whole or half squares. You can estimate the areas of these shapes by counting how many squares are more than half covered.

EXAMPLE:

4 squares are more than half covered by this boring purple blob.
So its area is about 4 cm².

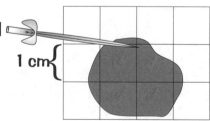

1 cm

ANOTHER EXAMPLE:

1 cm

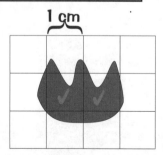

This footprint was left by a lesser spotted Cumbrian Yeti.
It has two squares that are more than half covered.
So its area is about 2 cm².

Learning Objective:

"I can draw a rectangle and work out its perimeter.
I can find the area of shapes by counting squares."

Calculating Perimeter and Area

Question 1

Draw a rectangle with a perimeter of **14 cm**.
Use the centimetre squared grid on the right.

1 You need to decide what length the sides will be. All rectangles have <u>two pairs</u> of <u>matching sides</u>.

2 Work out what the <u>long side</u> and the <u>short side</u> could be. A few different answers are possible.

3 <u>Draw</u> the rectangle on the grid.

Remember — use a ruler.

Long side + short side = half of 14 cm.
So long side + short side = 7 cm.

5 cm + 2 cm = 7 cm
So, long side = <u>5 cm</u>
short side = <u>2 cm</u>.

You could also have 4 cm + 3 cm or 6 cm + 1 cm.

5 cm | 2 cm | 2 cm | 5 cm

Question 2

Pete draws this shape on a centimetre squared grid. Find its approximate area.

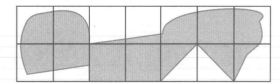

1 Count the number of squares that are <u>more than half covered</u>. <u>Number</u> each square as you count it.

2 Two squares are <u>exactly a half</u>. These will add together to make <u>1 whole square</u>.

3 Don't forget the <u>unit</u> — it's <u>cm²</u>.

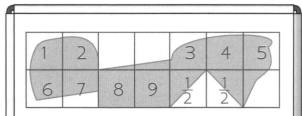

There are 9 squares more than half covered and two half squares. So the area is $9 + \frac{1}{2} + \frac{1}{2} = 10$ cm².

The area of a shape is measured in square units...

Yep, even if it's not a square. Just add all the 'more than half' squares together to get the total area. If there are half squares, you just add those together to make whole squares.

Units and Measures

Use Metric Units for Length

There are 4 units of length you need to know.

10 mm = 1 cm   100 cm = 1 m

1000 m = 1 km

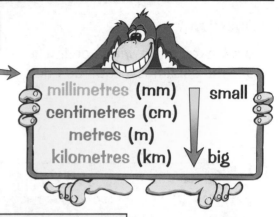

millimetres (mm)   small
centimetres (cm)
metres (m)
kilometres (km)   big

Use a Balance or Scales to Find Mass

You measure mass on a balance or weighing scales.
The units of mass are kilograms (kg) and grams (g).

Kilo means 1000 of something.
1 kilogram = 1000 grams

Capacity is How Much a Container Can Hold

Liquids have a volume. This is the amount of space they take up.
The largest volume of liquid something can hold is called its capacity.

You can measure capacity in
millilitres (ml) and litres (l).

"Milli" means $\frac{1}{1000}$.
There are 1000 millilitres in a litre.

Sometimes You Need to Convert Units

To convert a larger unit to a smaller unit you need to multiply.
You multiply by the number of smaller units that are in the bigger unit.

1 m = 100 cm

So to convert m to cm, multiply by 100.
EXAMPLE: 2 m = 2 × 100 = 200 cm

1 kg = 1000 g

So to convert kg to g, multiply by 1000.
EXAMPLE: 3.2 kg = 3.2 × 1000 = 3200 g

1 litre = 1000 ml

So to convert l to ml, multiply by 1000.
EXAMPLE: 0.4 l = 0.4 × 1000 = 400 ml

Learning Objective:

"I can choose appropriate units to
measure length, mass and capacity."

Units and Measures

Question 1

A grocer weighs a watermelon. The scales are marked in kg.
What is the mass of the watermelon in grams?

1 Find how much each 'jump' on the scale is worth.

There are 5 jumps between two numbered marks, so you know that each jump is: 1 kg ÷ 5 = 0.2 kg

2 Work out the mass of the watermelon in kilograms.

The arrow is 3 jumps on from 1 kg.
1 kg + 3 × 0.2 kg
= 1 + 0.6 = 1.6 kg

3 Convert the kilogram mass into grams to answer the question.

Multiply by 1000 to get the mass in g.
1.6 × 1000 = 1600 grams

Question 2

The lengths of three snakes are given below. Put the lengths in order from smallest to largest.

20.1 cm   1.8 m   1500 mm

1 You need to convert all the lengths to the same unit, say mm.

1 cm = 10 mm
So 20.1 cm = 20.1 × 10 mm = 201 mm

1 m = 100 cm
So 1.8 m = 1.8 × 100 cm = 180 cm
1 cm = 10 mm
So 180 cm = 180 × 10 mm = 1800 mm

2 Now put the lengths in mm in order.

The three lengths are:
    201 mm   1800 mm   1500 mm
In order, they are:
    201 mm   1500 mm   1800 mm

3 Now change each length back to the unit it was to begin with.

So,   20.1 cm   1500 mm   1.8 m

Weighing scales don't stop at fish...

If you have to put some measurements in order, make sure that they're all in the same unit first. Just convert all the measurements to the smallest unit by multiplying.

Practice Questions

1   The diagram on the right shows a plan of a garden.

What is the perimeter of the garden?

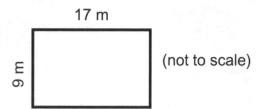

(not to scale)

2   A football pitch is 80 m long and 60 m wide. Helen walks all the way round the pitch.

How far does she walk?

3   Look at these rectangles.

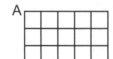 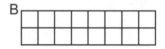

a)   Which of the rectangles has the largest perimeter?

b)   Which has the smallest area?

4   A gardener has 18 m of fence.
He wants to fence off a rectangle with the largest perimeter possible.

a)   Draw three different rectangles he could make on centimetre squared paper.
Use a scale of 1 cm : 1 m in your drawings.

b)   Use your drawings from part a) to work out which rectangle gives the **biggest area**.

5   Count the squares to find the areas of these shapes in square units.

a)

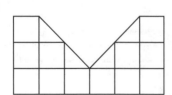

b)

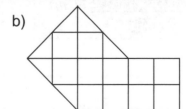

Practice Questions

6   Ribbon costs £2 per metre.
    Sarah needs ribbon to go around the edge of a box that is 2 m long and 1 m wide.

    How much will Sarah spend on ribbon?

7   Write these lengths in order, starting with the smallest.

    0.008 km   0.8 m   8000 cm

8   Elvis the hedgehog has a mass of 1.3 kg.
    Jemima the hedgehog has a mass of 1220 g.

    Which hedgehog has the greater mass?

9   Convert 2.5 kg into grams.

10 Circle one amount each time to make these sentences correct.

    a)   The height of a room is likely to be: 2 mm   2 cm   2 m

    b)   A saucepan is likely to hold about: 30 ml   3000 ml   30,000 ml

    c)   A pair of scissors is likely to weigh: 50 g   500 g   5000 g

11 Jake's bath holds 750 litres of water.

    How much is this in millilitres?

12 Sally has 1.5 litres of orange juice.

    How many 250 ml glasses can she fill?

1.5 litres

Analysing Data

The Mode is the Most Common Value

The <u>MODE</u> of a set of data is just the number that comes up <u>MOST</u> often.

To Work Out the Mode

1) Write all the numbers down in <u>order of size</u>.
2) Find the <u>number</u> that appears <u>most often</u> in your list.
3) This number is the <u>mode</u>.

EXAMPLE: Find the <u>mode</u> of this set of data:

10, 15, 5, 33, 15, 10, 15, 7

1) Rewrite the numbers <u>in order</u>: 5, 7, 10, 10, (15, 15, 15,) 33

2) The number <u>15</u> appears <u>3 times</u>. The other numbers
appear only <u>once</u> or <u>twice</u>. So <u>15</u> is the mode.

The Range is the Spread of the Data

The range of a set of data is the <u>difference</u> between the <u>biggest</u> and <u>smallest</u> numbers.

To Work Out the Range

1) Write all the numbers down in <u>order of size</u>.
2) <u>Subtract</u> the <u>smallest</u> number from the <u>biggest</u>.
3) This number is the <u>range</u>.

EXAMPLE: Find the <u>range</u> of this set of data:

7, 18, 8, 12, 15, 13, 6, 10

1) Rewrite the numbers <u>in order</u>: (6,) 7, 8, 10, 12, 13, 15, (18)

2) Subtract the <u>smallest number</u> from the <u>biggest number</u>: 18 − 6 = <u>12</u>

3) The range of the data is <u>12</u>.

Learning Objective:

"I can find the mode and the range of a set of data."

Analysing Data

Question 1

10 students take a Maths test. Their percentage scores are as follows:
84, 87, 77, 85, 87, 84, 85, 87, 72, 91. What score is the mode?

1 Write the numbers down in <u>order of size</u>.
It's a good idea to <u>cross them off</u> the list
so you don't miss any or write any twice.

2 Find the number that appears
<u>most often</u> in the list.

3 The number that appears most often is
the <u>mode</u>. And remember to answer the
question — here it's about a <u>% score</u>.

72, 77, 84, 84, 85, 85, 87, 87, 87, 91.

72 appears once.
77 appears once.
84 appears twice.
85 appears twice.
87 appears three times.
91 appears once.

Mode score = 87%

Question 2

Kevin measures the height of five of his friends in centimetres.
His results are: **131, 164, 149, 146** and **155**. What is the range of his data?

1 Write the numbers down
in <u>order of size</u>.

2 Subtract the <u>smallest number</u>
from the <u>biggest number</u>.

3 The answer to your calculation
is the <u>range</u> of the data.

131, 146, 149, 155, 164

$$\begin{array}{r} 164 \\ -131 \\ \hline 33 \end{array} \text{ cm}$$

Range = 33 cm

It's possible to have more than one mode...

Sometimes more than one number might be 'the most common' in a list. This is OK though.
In the list 2, 2, 4, 4, 5, 6, 7, the modes are 2 and 4, because they both appear twice.

Chance and Likelihood

Likelihood is How Likely an Event is to Happen

People talk about <u>chance</u> and <u>likelihood</u> a lot.

The weather forecast said it was very likely to rain.

It's possible there'll be thunder.

Broughton F.C. will probably beat Arsenal in the Cup on Saturday.

Unlikely, mate!

Here are <u>three words</u> people use when talking about likelihood:

<u>Impossible</u>
There's no chance at all of it happening.

<u>Uncertain</u>
Maybe it will happen, maybe it won't.

<u>Certain</u>
It'll definitely happen — no doubt about it.

You Can Estimate the Likelihood of Events

Some "uncertain" things have a <u>better chance</u> of happening than others.

→ Increasingly good chance →

| Impossible | <u>Unlikely</u> | Even chance | <u>Likely</u> | Certain |

Things that <u>aren't impossible</u> but have a <u>poor chance</u> of happening — such as it raining in a desert.

Things that are <u>equally likely</u> to happen as not to happen — like getting heads when you toss a coin.

Things that <u>aren't certain</u> but have a <u>good chance</u> of happening — such as it raining in England.

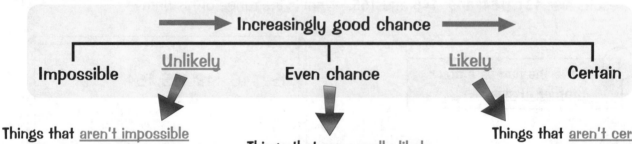

You are <u>likely</u> to get an <u>even number</u> on this spinner. That's because there are <u>more even numbers</u> than odd numbers.

There are eight numbers. Five of them are even. Only three are odd.

Learning Objective:

"I can describe how likely an event is to happen and justify my statement."

Chance and Likelihood

Question 1

How likely are the following events? Choose from the options below to answer.

certain   likely   even chance   unlikely   impossible

A   If I toss a coin, it will land on tails.
B   If I roll a normal dice, I will get a number between 1 and 6.
C   When I wake up tomorrow, I will be younger than I am today.

1   Think about the <u>possible outcomes</u> in each situation.

2   Then you can make a <u>better estimate</u> about the <u>likelihood</u> of the events happening.

A: A coin can land on heads OR tails. Both are just as likely to happen.
B: A normal dice is numbered 1 to 6.
C: People can't get younger. They can only get older.

A = Even chance
B = Certain
C = Impossible

Question 2

Jon uses this spinner to choose what colour socks he wears.
Decide whether these events are **likely**, **unlikely** or **impossible**:

1. Jon will wear red socks.   **2**. Jon will wear white socks.
3. Jon will wear pink socks.

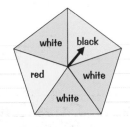

1   Look at the spinner. Write down <u>what colours</u> Jon can spin and <u>how likely</u> each one is.

2   Now you can say whether each event is <u>likely</u>, <u>unlikely</u> or <u>impossible</u>.

<u>White</u> is <u>quite likely</u>, because it takes up three of the five segments.

<u>Red</u> and <u>black</u> are <u>fairly unlikely</u> because they only take up one segment each.

Any other colour is <u>impossible</u>.

1.   Red socks = Unlikely
2.   White socks = Likely
3.   Pink socks = Impossible

Think about all the possible outcomes...

If you know all the different possibilities in a situation (e.g. a coin could either land on heads or tails) then it makes it easier to work out the chance of something happening.

Data

You Collect Data to Answer Questions

Data is just any set of facts or information.

You can collect data to help you answer questions. For example:

> On which morning is the road outside my school busiest?
>
> The data you would collect is the number of cars that go past each morning.
> Then you would be able to see which morning is the busiest.

Tally Marks are Good for Counting Things

Bert decides to count the cars going past his school each morning.
This tally chart shows how many cars he sees each day before 10am.

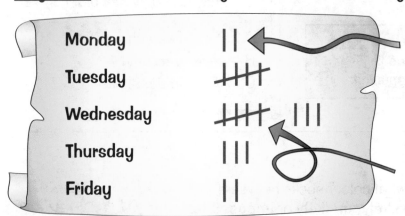

Each line shows one car that drives past.

When you have 4 lines together, the next line goes across them.
They stay in groups of 5.

You Can Turn Tally Charts into Frequency Tables

Tally marks aren't very easy to read.
It's easier to show the numbers in a frequency table.
You just count up the number of tally marks.

> Frequency means how many times something happens.

	Tally	Frequency
Monday	||	2
Tuesday	⊬	5
Wednesday	⊬ |||	8
Thursday	|||	3
Friday	||	2

Er...

Learning Objective:

"I can explain what a frequency chart tells me."

Data

Question 1

Tom asks his friends about their favourite type of holiday.
He collects their answers in a **frequency table**.

a) Fill in the gaps in Tom's table.
b) What kind of holiday is most popular?
c) What kind of holiday is least popular?
d) How many people did Tom ask altogether?

	Tally	Frequency
Beach	ⅢⅢ IIII	
Skiing		5
Safari		8
Cruise	ⅢⅢ ⅢⅢ III	
Sightseeing	II	2

a Use the <u>information already in the table</u> to fill in the gaps using either tally marks or numbers.

b The <u>most popular</u> type of holiday is the one with the <u>most tally marks</u> / <u>highest frequency</u>.

c The <u>least popular</u> type of holiday is the one with the <u>fewest tally marks</u> / <u>lowest frequency</u>.

d To find the <u>total number</u> of people Tom asked about holidays, add up all the numbers in the <u>'Frequency' column</u>.

a)

	Tally	Frequency
Beach	ⅢⅢ IIII	9
Skiing	ⅢⅢ	5
Safari	ⅢⅢ III	8
Cruise	ⅢⅢ ⅢⅢ III	13
Sightseeing	II	2

b) The most popular type of holiday is a cruise.
(<u>13</u> people said it was their favourite.)

c) The least popular is sightseeing.
(Only <u>2</u> people said it was their favourite.)

d) 9 + 5 + 8 + 13 + 2
= 37 people.

You can collect data to test predictions...

You might predict that the most common colour of car to drive past your school on Monday will be silver. You'd test this by tallying the different colours of cars you see driving past.

Tables and Charts

Pictograms are Numbers in Pictures

Pictograms use _pictures_ to show numbers of things or how often something happens. For example, Jamie counts how many times she rides the 'Monster Ride' in one week. She shows her data using a pictogram:

Monday

Tuesday

Wednesday

Thursday

Friday

= 2 goes on the Monster Ride

Jamie had three goes on the Monster Ride on Thursday.

Bar Charts Show Things at a Glance

Bar charts make it easy to _compare_ things.

The bars shouldn't touch each other.

Bar charts can also be called _block graphs_.

The _height_ of each bar shows how many times Jamie went on the ride.

Just _read across_ from the top of the bar to the number on the left.

For example, on _Thursday_ she went on the ride _3 times_.

Bar charts have two axes. This is the _horizontal axis_. The other is the _vertical axis_.

Learning Objective:

"I can show information in a bar chart or pictogram."

Tables and Charts

Question 1

Luke plays darts every day for five days.
He counts how many bull's-eyes he hits each day and makes a **pictogram**.

Work out how many bull's-eyes Luke hits each day.
Represent this information in a bar chart using the axes below.

Monday	◎ ◎
Tuesday	◖
Wednesday	◎ ◎ ◖
Thursday	◎ ◎ ◎ ◎
Friday	◎ ◎

◎ = 2 bull's-eyes

1 Use the <u>symbols</u> to work out how many bull's-eyes he hits each day.
Remember <u>1 dartboard</u> = <u>2 bull's-eyes</u>.

2 Add labels to the axes.
Put "Day of the week" on the <u>horizontal axis</u>.
Put "Number of bull's-eyes" on the <u>vertical axis</u>.

3 Use a ruler to <u>draw the bars</u> on your bar chart.
Make sure that they're <u>not touching</u>.

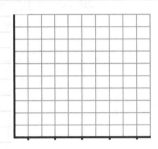

Monday = 4 bull's-eyes
Tuesday = 1 bull's-eye
Wednesday = 5 bull's-eyes
Thursday = 8 bull's-eyes
Friday = 4 bull's-eyes

Bar charts and pictograms both show frequency...

When you do a survey, you often make a frequency table. That's OK, but tables aren't a good way to <u>display</u> data. Bar charts and pictograms are good ways to show frequencies.

Tables and Charts

Drawing *Line Graphs*

Line graphs are a good way to show things that change over time — like distance or temperature.

Time	Speed
30 s	21 mph
60 s	75 mph
90 s	68 mph
120 s	33 mph

EXAMPLE: The table shows the speed of Zan the Genie at different times during an egg and spoon race. Plot the speeds on a line graph.

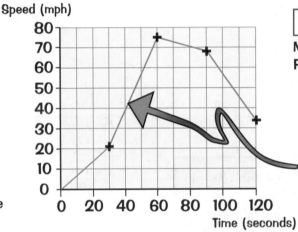

Step 1

Write a TITLE. Then draw and label the AXES.

Then number the axes. Go up in equal jumps (don't just put on the numbers from the table). And make sure that the biggest numbers in the table will fit on.

Step 2

Now draw a CROSS for each point. Find the time along the bottom and the speed up the side. Draw the cross where they meet.

Step 3

Then join the crosses with LINES. You don't know how Zan's speed changed between the crosses, so it's best to use STRAIGHT lines.

Reading *Line Graphs*

EXAMPLE: This line graph shows the temperature of Claire's oven one afternoon. Claire used the oven to bake a pie.

What was the temperature of the oven at 2:15?

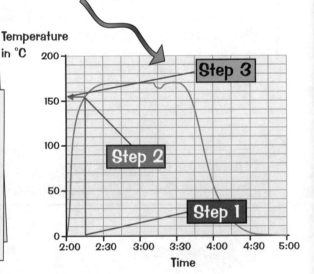

Step 1 Find 2:15 on the horizontal axis, then move STRAIGHT UP to the red line.

Step 2 Now look LEFT to the vertical axis.

Step 3 READ the value from the vertical axis.

It's halfway between 150 and 160 on the vertical axis, so the temperature was 155 °C.

Learning Objective:

"I can represent data using a line graph. I can explain the way I've represented data."

Tables and Charts

Question 1

A firework rocket was launched into the air.
This table shows its height at different times.

a) Plot the heights on a line graph.

b) Approximately how high was the rocket after 2.5 seconds?

c) Approximately how high was the rocket after 4.5 seconds?

Time	Height
0 s	0 m
1 s	25 m
2 s	40 m
3 s	45 m
4 s	40 m
5 s	25 m
6 s	0 m

a)

(1) Write a title, and draw and label the axes. Number the axes in equal jumps, making sure that the biggest height and time will fit on.

(2) Mark a cross on the graph for each pair of time and height measurements in the table. Join them up with straight lines using a ruler.

b) and c)

(1) Find the times in parts b) and c) on the horizontal axis. Move straight up to the red line. Then look left to the vertical axis.

(2) Read the values from the vertical axis to answer the questions. Remember to give the unit in your answer.

a) Graph to show the height of the firework

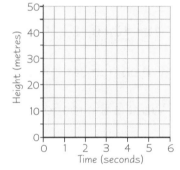

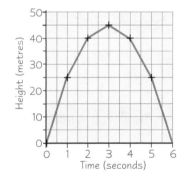

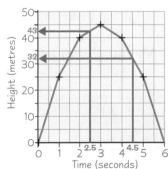

b) Approximately 43 m

c) Approximately 32 m

Graphs always tell the truth, even when they're line...

You can tell a lot from line graphs. If the line goes up, then the value on the vertical axis is increasing. If it goes down, it's decreasing. This makes it easy to spot patterns in data.

Practice Questions

1   Look at the shapes below.

What shape is the mode?

2   Look at the numbers below.

10, 10, 6, 2, 10, 5, 6, 2, 13, 10, 2, 1, 6

a)   Which number is the mode?

b)   What is the range of the numbers?

3   John measures the length in centimetres of each of his coloured pencils. His results are: 9, 12, 3, 14, 4, 5, 8, 13, 4, 10, 11, 6

What is the range of the lengths of his pencils?

4   Describe these events as **certain**, **likely**, **even chance**, **unlikely** or **impossible**.

a)   If I throw a normal dice, it will land on 6.

b)   If I jump in a swimming pool, I will get wet.

c)   My mum is younger than me.

5   Copy the probability scale below.

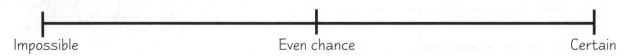

Draw arrows to show the likelihood of these events.

a)   Throwing a six on a normal dice.

b)   Throwing an odd number on a normal dice.

c)   Throwing a number greater than 4 on a normal dice.

Practice Questions

6   Brian records how many peas
    he eats each day for a week.

    a)   Copy and complete his table.

    b)   Draw a pictogram of Brian's data.
         Include a key. Use ⬤ to represent 4 peas.

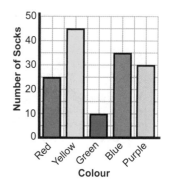

Day	Tally	Frequency
Monday	ⲙ̄ |||	
Tuesday		7
Wednesday	ⲙ̄ ⲙ̄ ⲙ̄ ⲙ̄ ||	
Thursday		13
Friday	|	
Saturday	ⲙ̄ |	
Sunday	||||	

7   The bar chart shows how many socks of each colour Mary has.

    a)   How many blue socks does Mary have?

    b)   Which colour is the mode?

    c)   How many socks does Mary have altogether?

8   Margaret plants a seed. It grows into a plant.
    She measures its height once a week for 7 weeks.

Week	1	2	3	4	5	6	7
Height (cm)	0	5	8	11	13	14	14

Draw a bar chart showing this information.

9   Gordon made some cakes on Sunday to sell in his shop.
    This line graph shows how many cakes he had left
    at closing time each day for the next week.

    a)   How many cakes were left at closing time on Tuesday?

    b)   How many cakes were sold on Saturday?

    c)   On which day did Gordon sell the largest number of cakes?

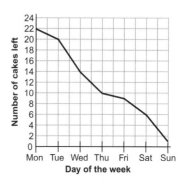

10 Emma measured the temperature in her greenhouse at
    hourly intervals one afternoon. Her results are shown below.

Time	1 pm	2 pm	3 pm	4 pm	5 pm
Temperature (°C)	50	44	30	26	22

Draw a line graph showing this data and use it to estimate the temperature at 3:30 pm.

Number Patterns

The most important thing about number sequences is finding a rule that links all the numbers. You can then use it to answer any question that is set.

Spot the Pattern to Complete a Sequence

EXAMPLE: What is the <u>next number</u> in the number sequence below?

| 2 | 5 | 11 | 23 | 47... |

You need to work out the rule that links the numbers...

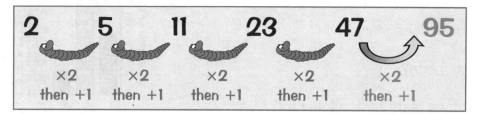

2   5   11   23   47   95

×2 then +1   ×2 then +1   ×2 then +1   ×2 then +1   ×2 then +1

Just double the last number in the pattern and add one.

Multiples Also Follow Patterns

EXAMPLE:

$$0 + 9 = 9$$
$$9 + 9 = 18$$
$$18 + 9 = \boxed{27}$$
$$27 + 9 = 36$$
$$36 + 9 = 45$$

Every time you add 9 the <u>tens</u> go <u>up 1</u> and the <u>units</u> go <u>down 1</u> (till you get to 90).

e.g. 4 + 5 = 9

18
+ 1   − 1
27

The digits in multiples of 9 always <u>add up to 9</u> (or a multiple of 9) too.

There are other multiples with patterns like this:

$$4 \times 5 = 20$$
$$5 \times 5 = 25$$
$$6 \times 5 = 30$$
$$7 \times 5 = 35$$
$$8 \times 5 = 40$$

Multiples of 5 end in 0 or 5

$$4 \times 10 = 40$$
$$5 \times 10 = 50$$
$$6 \times 10 = 60$$
$$7 \times 10 = 70$$
$$8 \times 10 = 80$$

Multiples of 10 end in 0

Another pattern is that <u>any multiple</u> of an <u>even number</u> will <u>end in an even number</u> or <u>zero</u>.

Learning Objective:

"I can see number patterns and can explain how the pattern works."

Number Patterns

Question 1

Work out the next two numbers in the following number sequence:

1, 2, 5, 14, 41...

1 Have a look at the difference between each number in the sequence. Work out the <u>rule</u> that links the numbers.

2 When you've worked out the pattern, apply it to the <u>last number in the sequence</u>.

3 <u>Continue the sequence</u> as far as you have to.

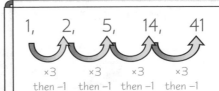

1,   2,   5,   14,   41

×3   ×3   ×3   ×3
then −1   then −1   then −1   then −1

41 × 3 − 1 = 122
122 × 3 − 1 = 365

1, 2, 5, 14, 41, 122, 365
The next two numbers are
<u>122</u> and <u>365</u>.

Question 2

Fill in the boxes so that the answer to the calculation is a multiple of 5.
Use the numbers **8**, **2**, **9** and **8**.

□□ − □□ = ?

1 First of all, think about any <u>patterns</u> you know that relate to <u>multiples of 5</u>.

2 <u>Apply this pattern</u> to the numbers you've been given.

3 Then you can <u>write in the other numbers</u> to complete the calculation.

Multiples of 5 can only end in 0 or 5.

So the units must subtract to give 0 or 5:

     8 − 2 = 6
     9 − 8 = 1
     9 − 2 = 7
     8 − 8 = 0.
So use the 8s as units.

□8 − □8 =

9 8 − 2 8 = 7 0

It's like playing spot the difference...

Tackle these questions by writing down the differences until you can see the pattern.
It'll be really helpful if you can remember the rules for spotting multiples too.

Number Patterns

Each Number in a _Sequence_ is Called a _Term_

EXAMPLE: Paul the lazy builder is building a wall. He lays 4 bricks on day 1. Then he adds 3 bricks every day.

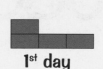   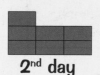

1st day   2nd day   3rd day

Paul says, "By the end of the 6th day, the wall will have 20 bricks." <u>Is he right</u>?

Write out the <u>number of bricks in the wall</u> each day as terms in a <u>sequence</u>.

4, 7, 10, ...   You're <u>adding 3</u> more bricks each day.

So just keep adding 3 until you get to the <u>6th</u> term. ⟶ 4, 7, 10, 13, 16, 19, ...
By the end of the 6th day the wall will have 19 bricks.
So Paul is <u>wrong</u>.

Symbols _Stand in for_ Numbers You Don't Know

You can use <u>letters</u> or <u>pictures</u> to stand in for numbers. For example, h could mean a <u>height</u>. You could use ◯ to represent the <u>cost of one custard pie</u>, in pence.

Then... Two custard pies would cost 2◯ pence.
Three custard pies would cost 3◯ pence...

2◯ means 2 × ◯.
(And 5h means 5 × h.)

EXAMPLE:

Mike sees this sign and buys 5 custard pies.
He says, "The total cost in pence will be 5◯ – 50."
If ◯ = 70, how much does Mike pay?

Special Offer
Buy 5 CUSTARD PIES,
get 50p off!

<u>ANSWER:</u> You have to work out <u>5 × ◯</u>, then <u>subtract 50</u>.
◯ = 70, so it's <u>5 × 70</u> = 350, 350 <u>– 50</u> = 300

So Mike pays <u>300p</u> (or <u>£3</u>).

Learning Objective:

"I can describe and explain patterns, sequences and relationships."

Number Patterns

Question 1

Laura writes a number sequence. The rule to get to the next number is to
add three and then multiply by 2. The sequence contains the number 506.
What is the number immediately **before 506** in Laura's sequence?

① To find the number <u>before</u> 506, you need to <u>reverse the rule</u>.

② Now you've found the reverse rule you can <u>apply it to 506</u> to find the number before it in the sequence.

The opposite of + 3 then × 2 is:
÷ 2 and then − 3

So reversing the rule gives you:
506 ÷ 2 =   253
And 253 − 3 =   250

So the number before 506
in the sequence = 250.

Question 2

 Find the missing numbers in the following sequence. The rule is **subtract** .
The sequence is 5.1, ☐ , ☐ , ☐ , ☐ , 2.1.

① Find the <u>difference</u> between the first and last number.

② Count how many <u>steps</u> there are between the first and last number.

③ <u>Divide</u> the difference by the number of steps.

④ Now you know the subtraction at each step, <u>fill in the missing numbers</u>.

Subtract 2.1 from 5.1 :
5.1 − 2.1 =   3

▲ has been subtracted 5 times from the first to last number.

So the subtraction at each step is:
▲ = 3 ÷ 5 = 0.6

So the missing numbers are:
-0.6 -0.6 -0.6 -0.6 -0.6

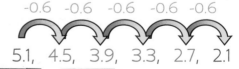

Follow the rule — you just have to find it first...

You've got to work out the rule before you can answer any question on number patterns.
Practise the examples until you can remember the steps involved.

Practice Questions

1   Look at the numbers in this sequence: 5   12   26   54   110

What is the rule to get from one number to the next?

2   A sequence starts: 1   4   13   40

   a)   What is the rule for finding the next term?

   b)   What is the 6th number in this sequence?

3   The rule for a pattern is "multiply by 3 and add 5".
The pattern starts with 1.

What are the next three numbers?

4   Fill in the missing numbers in this sequence.

26, 23, ☐, 17, ☐, ☐, 8, 5, ☐

5   A farmer has 4 sheep in a field.
Every week, he buys 5 more sheep and puts them in the same field.

If no sheep leave the field, how many sheep will there be after 3 weeks?

6   Jim runs a fruit shop.
Bananas cost **b** pence each. Coconuts cost **c** pence each.

   a)   How much would **8 bananas** cost?

   b)   Jim writes this number sentence to work out the total cost of some shopping in pence:

      3c + 20

      If c = 90, what is the total cost of the shopping in pence?

Practice Questions

7 Look at this sequence: 2.1, , 4.1, ...

The rule for this sequence is "add ▲".
Find the missing numbers in the sequence.

8 Write one of these digits in each box to make a sequence where the rule is "add 9".

1, 1, 2, 2, 3, 3, 4

☐ , ☐☐ , ☐☐ , ☐☐

9 Draw the next 2 shapes in this sequence.

10 Here are the first 3 shapes in a sequence.

Shape 1   Shape 2   Shape 3

  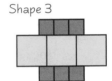

a) Fill in the following table.

Shape Number	1	2	3	4
Number of Yellow Squares				
Number of Red Squares				

b) What is the rule for yellow squares?

c) What is the rule for red squares?

11 Ellen makes a sequence of patterns using matchsticks.

Pattern 1   Pattern 2   Pattern 3   Pattern 4

How many matchsticks will be in the 8th pattern in the sequence?

12 Every month, the number of rabbits in a hutch doubles.

There were 3 rabbits in the hutch to start with.
How many rabbits will there be after 3 months?

Section Seven — Using and Applying Mathematics

Answers

Pages 10-11 — Section One

1) $2.658 = \mathbf{2} + \mathbf{0.6} + \mathbf{0.05} + \mathbf{0.008}$

2) Michael's time = 14.45 s + 0.1 s = **14.55 s**

3) a) 0.14

   b)
   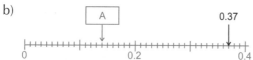

4) 6.01 has the largest unit so put it at the end. All the rest have the same tenths value so look at the hundredths. 5.9<u>9</u> is larger than 5.9<u>32</u> or 5.9<u>30</u>, so put it second to last. 5.93<u>0</u> is less than 5.93<u>2</u>, so 5.930 goes first. The order is: **5.930 s, 5.932 s, 5.99 s, 6.01 s**
   For help with putting numbers in order look at the pages on DECIMALS.

5)

   Jeremy's score was higher by **3 points**.

6) a) $6 > 2$ b) $-3 < -1$ c) $2.3 < 2.5$

7)
   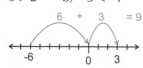
   The temperature difference is **9 °C**

8) $\dfrac{8}{10} = \dfrac{80}{100} = \mathbf{80\%}$

9) Convert the percentage into a fraction, or the fraction into a percentage.

   $\dfrac{1}{4} = 25\%$. 25% is greater than 20%.

   OR, $20\% = \dfrac{20}{100} = \dfrac{1}{5}$. $\dfrac{1}{4}$ is greater than

   $\dfrac{20}{100} = \dfrac{1}{5}$.

   So **Katherine** ate more porridge.

10) 2 out of every 3 socks are blue.

   So $\dfrac{2}{3}$ of the socks are blue.

   $\dfrac{2}{3}$ of 60 socks = **40 socks**

   If you need help, have a look at the pages on PROPORTION AND RATIO.

11) One egg costs $90 \div 3 = 30$p.
   4 eggs cost 4×30 p = **120 p** or **£1.20**

12) a) $12 \div 3 = \mathbf{4\ cakes}$
   b) 36 is three times 12.
   So he needs 3 times the amount of margarine.
   3×75 g = **225 g**

Pages 20-21 — Section Two

1) $239 + 731 = 970$
   $229 + 731 = 960$
   Jason is correct.

2) 59×11 is about the same as 60×10.
   $60 \times 10 = 600$. Mildred's answer is much bigger than 600, so she is **probably wrong**.
   For some help, look at the pages on CHECKING CALCULATIONS.

3) 9 cm + 5 cm = 14 cm. He has used the wrong units in his answer.

4) 35. It's less than 50 <u>and</u> a multiple of 5 so it should be in the overlap part of the diagram.

5) a) 12 or 15
   b) 16 or 56

6) 18, 54 and 72

7) 33

8) a) 72
   b) 8
   c) 6

9) 5×9 seats = 45 seats. So **45 people** can go.

10) a) $108 \div 9 = ?$
   $12 \times 9 = 108$, so **12 boxes**
   b) 6×9 chocolates = **54 chocolates**

11) $64 \div 8 = \mathbf{8\ packs}$ of jam tarts

12) $60 \div 7 = ?$
   $8 \times 7 = 56$, $9 \times 7 = 63$.
   So Daphne has enough beads to make
   8 necklaces. (She'll have 4 beads left over.)

13) Yes he is right. 36 is 6^2.

   6×6 grid has 36 squares

14) $4^2 = 4 \times 4 = 16$ $7^2 = 7 \times 7 = 49$
   $49 - 16 = 33$
   So Ellen has **33 more** stickers than Amy.

15) $60^2 = 6^2 \times 10^2 = 36 \times 100 = \mathbf{3600}$
   Remember, $60^2 = 6^2 \times 10^2$, not $6^2 \times 10$.
   If you need help, have a look at the pages on SQUARE NUMBERS.

16) $80^2 = 8^2 \times 10^2 = 64 \times 100 = \mathbf{6400}$ Maths books

Pages 34-35 — Section Three

1) $42 \times 10 = \mathbf{420\ bananas}$

2) $220 \div 10 = \mathbf{22\ people}$
   If you multiply by 10 or 100 the digits move to the left. If you divide by 10 or 100 the digits move to the right. Take another look at the pages on MULTIPLY AND DIVIDE BY 10 AND 100 if you need help with this.

3) $22 + 56 = \mathbf{78\ vehicles}$

Answers

4) $150 - 69 = 150 - 70 + 1 = 80 + 1 = $ **81 girls**

5)
```
   7643
+  6391
  14034
    ₁₁
```
So **14 034** people went to the matches.

6) a)
```
£ 2 . 7 |5|   £|3| . 9 9   £ 1 0 . 1 |2|
£ 4 . 9 9   £ 2 . 0 0   £   |4| . 1 3
£|7| . 7 4   £ 5 . 9 |9|   £ 1 4 . 2 5
```
   b) $£7.74 + £5.99 + £14.25 = $ **£27.98**

7)
```
   ₁ ₁₃
   2̸3̸8
 − 1 5 4
     8 4
```
So **84** sweets are left.

8)
```
   ⁵ ¹¹ ¹
   1̸6̸.2̸5
 −   2.68
    13.57
```
So Henry has **£13.57 left**.

9)
```
    9.79        ₁ ⁹ ⁹
 +  3.49      £ 2̸0̸.0̸0
   13.28    − £ 1 3 . 2 8
    ₁ ₁      £   6 . 7 2
```
So Dave will get **£6.72 change**.

10)
```
   127
 ×   3
   381
     ₂
```
$£381 + £32.50 = £413.50$

```
    ⁷¹ ₂ ₁
   15̸8̸3̸.00
 −   413.50
   1169.50
```
So the charity still needs to raise **£1169.50**

11) a)
```
     16
 ×   25
     80
 + 3₃20
    ₁
    400
    ₁
```
   400 beans in one box
   b) 400 beans × 3 = **1200 beans**
   If you need help, take a look at the WRITTEN MULTIPLYING AND DIVIDING pages.

12) a)
```
   7)163
 −  140   (7 × 20)
     23
 −   21   (7 × 3)
      2
```
   There will be **23** flowers in a bunch.
   b) There will be **2 flowers left over**.

13)   60p × 6 = 360p = £3.60
      £1.20 × 4 = £4.80
      £3.60 + £4.80 = **£8.40**

14)   Cost of 3 pairs of socks = £2.99 × 3 = £8.97
      Cost of 2 hats = £5.89 × 2 = £11.78
      Total cost = £8.97 + £11.78 = £20.75
      £25 − £20.75 = **£4.25 change**

Pages 46-47 — Section Four

1)   quadrilateral
2)   **A** and **D** — they are the only triangles with 2 equal sides and 2 equal angles.
3) a) 8   (2 end faces and 6 joining faces)
   b) 12
4) a) cuboid / rectangular prism
   b) tetrahedron / triangle based pyramid
   c) (pentagonal) prism
5)   E.g.

6)   E.g.

7) a) acute
   b) 60°
   Acute angles are less than 90°. Check out the pages on ANGLES if you need some help.

8)

9) a) (7, 3)
   b) (6, 8)
10) Work out the side length of the squares using the x- or y-coordinates.
     $4 - 1 = 3$ (or $5 - 2 = 3$)
     The side length of both squares is 3.
     So the coordinates of point A must be
     $(5 + 3, 4 + 3) = (8, 7)$.
     Penny's y-coordinate is wrong.
     This isn't a nice one. If you need help, look at the pages on COORDINATES.

11)

12) Shapes B, C, D and E.

Answers

Pages 52-53 — Section Five

1) 17 m + 9 m + 17 m + 9 m = **52 m**
2) 80 m + 60 m + 80 m + 60 m = **280 m**
3) a) Rectangle **B** (It has a perimeter of 20.
    The others have a perimeter of 16.)
   b) Rectangle **A** (It has an area of 15 squares.
    The others have an area of 16 squares.)

4) a)

```
      8 cm
 ┌──────────────┐ 1 cm
 └──────────────┘

      7 cm
 ┌────────────┐ 2 cm
 │            │
 └────────────┘

      6 cm
 ┌──────────┐ 3 cm
 │          │
 │          │
 └──────────┘

    5 cm
 ┌────────┐ 4 cm
 │        │
 │        │
 │        │
 └────────┘
```

   b) Area of an 8 m by 1 m rectangle
    = 8 m × 1 m = 8 m²
    Area of a 7 m by 2 m rectangle
    = 7 m × 2 m = 14 m²
    Area of a 6 m by 3 m rectangle
    = 6 m × 3 m = 18 m²
    Area of a 5 m by 4 m rectangle
    = 5 m × 4 m = 20 m²
    A **5 m by 4 m** rectangle has the biggest area.
5) a) 14 square units
   b) 14 square units
6) Perimeter of box:
    2 m + 1 m + 2 m + 1 m = 6 m.
    So Sarah needs 6 m of ribbon.
    Total cost = 6 × £2 = **£12**.
    If you need help, look at the pages on
    CALCULATING PERIMETER AND AREA.
7) Change them all into the same unit, for
    example, metres:
    0.008 × 1000 = 8 m
    8000 ÷ 100 = 80 m
    0.8 m, 0.008 km, 8000 cm
8) 1.3 kg = 1300 g. **Elvis** has the larger mass.
9) 2.5 × 1000 = **2500 g**
10)a) 2 m
   b) 3000 ml
   c) 50 g
11) 750 × 1000 = **750 000 ml**
12) 1.5 l = 1500 ml
    1500 ml ÷ 250 ml = 6
    So Sally can fill **6 glasses**.
    If you need some help changing between units,
    look at the UNITS AND MEASURES pages.

Pages 64-65 — Section Six

1) ○
2) a) The data in size order:
    1, 2, 2, 2, 5, 6, 6, 6, 10, 10, 10, 10, 13
    The mode is **10**.
   b) 13 − 1 = **12**
    The mode is the most common value.
    For help with finding the mode and range of
    data, see the pages on ANALYSING DATA.
3) 3, 4, 4, 5, 6, 8, 9, 10, 11,12, 13, 14
    So the range = 14 − 3 = **11**
4) a) unlikely
   b) certain
   c) impossible

5)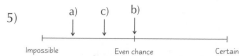

6) a)

Day	Tally	Frequency
Monday	IIII III	8
Tuesday	IIII II	7
Wednesday	IIII IIII IIII IIII II	22
Thursday	IIII IIII III	13
Friday	I	1
Saturday	IIII I	6
Sunday	IIII	4

   b) E.g

Monday	●●
Tuesday	●◔
Wednesday	●●●●●◗
Thursday	●●●◖
Friday	◗
Saturday	●◗
Sunday	●

KEY: ● = 4 peas

7) a) 35
   b) Yellow
   c) 25 + 45 + 10 + 35 + 30 = **145**

8) E.g.

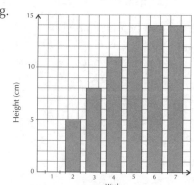

Answers

9) a) 20 cakes
   b) Find the difference between closing time on Friday and closing time on Saturday.
      Friday = 9 cakes
      Saturday = 6 cakes. 9 – 6 = **3 cakes**.
   c) **Wednesday**. (The difference between closing time on Tuesday and closing time on Wednesday is the greatest on the graph.)
10) E.g.

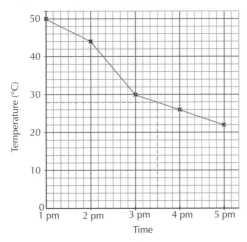

Reading from the graph, the temperature at 3:30 is **28 °C**.
Whenever you're drawing charts or graphs, make sure you use a sensible scale. Check out the TABLES AND CHARTS pages.

Pages 70-71 — Section Seven

1) multiply by 2 then add 2
2) a) multiply by 3 then add 1
   b) 5th term: 40 × 3 = 120. 120 + 1 = 121
      6th term: 121 × 3 = 363. 363 + 1 = **364**
      If you need some help, check out the pages on NUMBER PATTERNS.
3) 2nd term: 1 × 3 = 3. 3 + 5 = **8**
   3rd term: 8 × 3 = 24. 24 + 5 = **29**
   4th term: 29 × 3 = 87. 87 + 5 = **92**
4) The rule is subtract three.
   26, 23, **20**, 17, **14**, **11**, 8, 5, **2**
5) The rule is add 5.
   Week 1: 4 + 5 = 9 sheep
   Week 2: 9 + 5 = 14 sheep
   Week 3: 14 + 5 = 19 sheep
   So there will be **19** sheep in the field.
6) a) 8b
   b) 3c + 20 = 3 × 90 + 20 = 270 + 20 = 290.
      So the total cost is **290p**.

7) 4.1 – 2.1 = 2
   There are 4 steps so 4 × 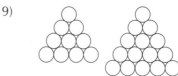 = 2
   So ▲ = 2 ÷ 4 = 0.5.
   So the rule is add 0.5
   The sequence is 2.1, **2.6**, **3.1**, **3.6**, 4.1
   Don't let the symbol in this question worry you. It's just a 'find the rule' type question. If you need some help, have a look at the NUMBER PATTERNS pages.
8) 4, 13, 22, 31
   (The tens increase by 1 and the units decrease by 1.)
9)

10)a)

Shape Number	1	2	3	4
Number of Yellow Squares	1	2	3	4
Number of Red Squares	2	4	6	8

   b) add 1
   c) add 2
11) The rule is add 2.
   3, 5, 7, 9, 11, 13, 15, 17
   The 8th pattern will be made up of **17** matchsticks.
12) Month 1: 3 × 2 = 6
   Month 2: 6 × 2 = 12
   Month 3: 12 × 2 = 24
   There will be **24** rabbits after 3 months.

Index